D1562660

What Makes Charity Work?

WHAT MAKES CHARITY WORK?

A Century of Public and Private Philanthropy

EDITED WITH AN INTRODUCTION BY
MYRON MAGNET

CHICAGO   *Ivan R. Dee*   2000

The contents of this book first appeared in *City Journal*, published by The Manhattan Institute.

Library of Congress Cataloging-in-Publication Data:
What makes charity work? : a century of public and private philanthropy / edited with an introduction by Myron Magnet.
    p. cm.
   Includes index.
   ISBN 1-56663-334-6 (alk. paper)
    1. Charities—United States. 2. Public welfare—United States.
  I. Magnet, Myron.

HV91 .W493 2000
361.2'0973—dc21   00-034563

Contents

MYRON MAGNET

Introduction

FORTY YEARS AGO, more or less, our commonly accepted notions of charity—and of the compassion of which charity is the practical expression—went through a momentous transformation. The change was crucial for the nation's intellectual and moral life, not only because charity has traditionally been at the center of what constitutes our duty to our fellows and our sense of obligation both religious and civic, but also because charity and compassion, having survived the culture wars that reduced so many traditional beliefs and values to smoking ruins, came to loom all the larger in a moral landscape that was otherwise so flat. More important still, the change in our idea of charity has had enormous political and social repercussions as well, providing a rationale for the vast expansion in America's welfare state and a corresponding shrinkage of the realm of civil society.

Introduction

Today our conception of charity seems once again in the process of revision. As evidence, consider the 1996 welfare reform act and the provision that act contains to allow religious organizations, without disguising their religious character, to provide social services under government contract. Consider the 2000 presidential campaign's debate over what constitutes the compassion in "compassionate conservatism" and how that compassion should be translated into action. And consider as well the intense journalistic interest that surrounds the new philanthropic ventures of the baby-boom billionaires, newly minted by Wall Street and the computer and Internet industries.

Much is at stake, therefore, in what results from the revision now under way. For that reason, this is an ideal moment to assess just how the theory and practice of charity has evolved in modern American life, and with what consequences. That is what this collection of essays from *City Journal*—which regularly reports on these developments—undertakes to do: to look back over the last century and more to see where we have come from, and to look forward to understand what we should do now.

Until the 1960s a broad consensus reigned in American charity. In only some cases, the theory went, was need a merely material question: from time to time, a sober workman might need cash assistance while recovering from illness or injury, for example, or a widow might need tiding over until she could find work. But by and large, charity was much more than the handing out of cash. Philanthropy in the nineteenth and early twentieth centuries concentrated on education and acculturation, on moral reclamation and rehabilitation—on turning lives around and getting people on the right track. It cared as much for the mind and soul as for the body. Abhorring the idea of dependency, it aimed to make its beneficiaries self-sufficient. Unwilling to leave the poor marginalized, it sought instead to bring them into the mainstream, to make them fully American, fully working class or, whenever possible, middle class.

Traditional American charity, therefore, stressed the skills and the attitudes of self-reliance and personal responsibility. Their absence, philanthropists believed, was the principal cause of chronic poverty. Charity focused on sparking an inner change in the recipient. It did not believe that a poor man was simply a man without money, whose problems could be solved by a handout. Instead charity sought to inculcate the missing—and crucial—virtues and skills that would allow its recipients to succeed on their own, to take advantage of the manifold opportunities that American society provided.

Emphatically values-laden, traditional charity frequently was explicitly religious, even sectarian, and some of the chapters that follow chronicle some representative examples of such philanthropic enterprises. But the secular and nondenominational charities of the generations before the 1960s share a very similar spirit. All, religious and secular, strove to inculcate the same self-examination, the same bourgeois morality, the same habits of personal responsibility. All believed that the chronically poor were too often poor because of their own self-destructive behavior and defeatist worldview. So whether they saw themselves as saving souls or just helping people turn their lives around through right habits and right living, their practical messages were broadly similar.

And these charities were remarkably successful, even with social problems that were no less dauntingly severe than those we face today. As the two stories by William J. Stern at the start of this volume show, America had an underclass long before the one we have today: the Irish. Among them, drunkenness, prostitution, illegitimacy, violence, and crime were epidemic in the second half of the nineteenth century, and were much more often the cause, rather than the effect, of their unimaginable poverty. Tens of thousands of abandoned, unsocialized Irish kids roamed the streets of New York, ripe for trouble. Yet within the space of a generation, the Catholic charities of New York brought about an extraordinary transformation, and by the end of the century most New York Irish were firmly within the mainstream of American life. Howard Husock's chapter shows how, from the perspective of a single individual's experience, traditional charities—in this case, a Jewish rather than a Catholic one—achieved their notable and profoundly inspiring successes.

With the 1960s everything changed, and the chapters by Heather Mac Donald and Brian C. Anderson trace that change as it affected some of the nation's key philanthropies, secular and religious alike. The *New York Times*'s Hundred Neediest Cases appeal, Mac Donald shows, and the great philanthropic foundations that have done so much to reshape our national life began as traditional charities, based on traditional principles. But the cultural revolution of the sixties changed their character utterly. No longer did these institutions see the personal behavior and worldview of the poor as the key to the improvement of their condition. Now, consistent with the elite orthodoxy of the age, they ascribed poverty to much larger forces: to an unjust economy and a racist society, to "the system," which consigned some to failure regardless of their good morals, upright behavior, and willingness to abide by the rules.

Philanthropy now became a wholesale rather than a retail enterprise, concentrating not on individuals but on an abstract Mankind and on the all-embracing system that purportedly misshaped so many lives. Charitable projects became gigantic in their scale and ambition. At the center of all of them stood government. It could right economic injustice by redistributing income through massive welfare programs. And it could right social injustices by schemes of social engineering that proliferated all the more plentifully in the wake of failure after failure, always explained away by the assertion that the failed programs didn't go far enough. So the role of organized charities was now to become advocates for social and economic change brought about by government: through gargantuan public housing projects; through government-sponsored programs in the schools that created self-esteem in the poor and marginalized; through ever vaster and more generous government-funded programs ministering to a growing catalog of needs, from prenatal services to unmarried pregnant teens to hospices for homeless, drug-addicted AIDS victims. And, of course, through class-action lawsuits that forced governments to do more and more of the same.

Henceforth anyone who sought to help the poor as individuals, one by one, looked hopelessly naive, as if trying to empty the sea with a spoon. And anyone who tried to distinguish among the poor, separating the bums and crooks from those trying to live upright lives and improve their condition by effort, sacrifice, and self-restraint, appeared, worse still, heartless and cruel. Distinguishing the deserving from the undeserving poor was an anachronistic, Victorian error, based on the sadly unsophisticated belief that individual action and striving make any difference in the face of the insuperable, undiscriminating forces of inequality and injustice. Making such distinctions would be merely "blaming the victim," as the then-trendy cant had it. Enlightened philanthropy would now spend private dollars to persuade government to spend much vaster amounts of the taxpayers' money to create a social environment in which all would flourish.

Especially compared with the successes of traditional

philanthropy, the results of the new charity were disappointing in the extreme. (Heather Mac Donald details the full extent of this failure in a companion volume, *The Burden of Bad Ideas*.) After more than $5 trillion of government welfare spending, the condition of the long-term poor is no better than when the mighty effort of advocacy and uplift began. If anything, the new philanthropy left the chronic poor worse off than before, for it delegitimized all the effective principles of traditional charity and traditional self-help. In addition, it corrupted many powerful philanthropic institutions, from the Ford Foundation to Catholic Charities USA, so that instead of being part of the solution, they became part of the problem.

Fortunately America is a proverbially practical nation, quick to learn from experience; and Americans have begun to recognize and to mull over the failure of the government programs that the new philanthropy stimulated. They have begun to lose confidence in the assumptions that inspired the programs and in the advocates who lobbied for them—though that has been a painful experience for many, whose sense of their own moral excellence has depended on their belief in their superior compassion, as manifested by their support for all the government programs once thought to be compassion's embodiment. Still, the nation tried the experiments the advocates recommended, and Americans have assessed the dismal results and have judged accordingly.

The first consequence of that reassessment is welfare reform: if you are doing something that doesn't work—that probably even makes things worse—the prudent course is to *stop* doing it. But then what?

The essays by Sol Stern and Kay S. Hymowitz that close this volume sketch out an answer to that question. Some charities have begun to return to the old model of helping the poor one by one, concerned with changing their behavior and turning around their lives. The results have been impressively positive and well worth pondering. Drawing on the experience-tested wisdom of the past, they point a workable way forward, one that the nation is likely to follow soon.

What Makes Charity Work?

William J. Stern

How Dagger John Saved New York's Irish

WE ARE NOT the first generation of New Yorkers puzzled by what to do about the underclass. A hundred years ago and more, Manhattan's tens of thousands of Irish seemed a lost community, mired in poverty and ignorance, destroying themselves through drink, idleness, violence, criminality, and illegitimacy. What made the Irish such miscreants? Their neighbors weren't sure: perhaps because they were an inferior race, many suggested; you could see it in the shape of their heads, writers and cartoonists often emphasized. In any event, they were surely incorrigible.

But within a generation, New York's Irish flooded into the American mainstream. The sons of criminals were now the policemen; the daughters of illiterates had become the city's schoolteachers; those who'd been the outcasts of society now ran its political machinery. No job-training program or welfare system brought about so sweeping a change. What accomplished it, instead, was a moral transformation, a revolution in values. And just as John Wesley, the founder of Methodism in the late eighteenth century, had sparked a change in the culture of the English working class that made it unusually industrious and virtuous, so too a clergyman was the catalyst for the cultural change that liberated New York's Irish from their underclass behavior. He was John Joseph Hughes, an Irish immigrant gardener who became the first Catholic archbishop of New York. How he accomplished his task can teach us volumes about the solution to our own end-of-the-millennium social problems.

John Hughes's personal history embodied all the virtues he tried so successfully to inculcate in his flock. They were very much the energetic rather than the contemplative virtues: as a newspaper reporter of the time remarked of him, he was "more a Roman gladiator than a devout follower of the meek founder of Christianity." He was born on June 24, 1797, in Annaloghan, County Tyrone, the son of a poor farmer. As a Catholic in English-ruled Ireland, he was, he said, truly a second-class citizen from the day he was baptized, barred from ever owning a house worth more than five pounds or holding a commission in the army or navy. Catholics could neither run schools nor give their children a Catholic education. Priests had to be licensed by the government, which allowed only a few in the country. Any Catholic son could seize his father's property by becoming a Protestant.

When Hughes was fifteen, an event he was never to forget crystallized for him the injustice of English domination. His younger sister, Mary, died. English law barred the local Catholic priest from entering the cemetery gates to preside at her burial; the best he could do was to scoop up a handful of dirt, bless it, and hand it to Hughes to sprinkle on the grave. From early on, Hughes said, he had dreamed of "a country in which no stigma of inferiority would be impressed on my brow, simply because I professed one creed or another."

Fleeing poverty and persecution, Hughes's father brought the family to America in 1817. The twenty-year-old Hughes went to work as a gardener and stonemason at Mount St. Mary's college and seminary in Emmitsburg, Maryland. Working there rekindled in him a childhood dream of becoming a priest, and he asked the head of the seminary, John Dubois, if he could enroll as a student. Dubois, a French priest who had fled Paris during the French Revolution armed with a letter of recommendation from Lafayette, turned him down, unable to see past his lack of education to the qualities of mind and character that lay within. This was no ordinary gardener, Dubois should have recognized; indeed, as he went back to his gardening chores, Hughes wrote a bitter poem on the shamefulness of slavery and its betrayal of America's promise of freedom. Not one to forget a slight, Hughes harshly froze Dubois out of his life when he became prominent and powerful. Indeed, in later years, Hughes won the nickname of "Dagger John," a reference not only to the shape of the cross that accompanied his printed signature but also to his being a man not to be trifled with or double-crossed.

With the good luck that marked his career, Hughes met Mother Elizabeth Bayley Seton, who visited Mount St. Mary's from time to time, and impressed her deeply with all those talents that Dubois had failed to see. A Protestant convert to Rome who had become a nun after her New York blueblood husband died, Mother Seton was a powerful influence on American Catholicism and was canonized as America's first and only native-born saint after her death. When she wrote to

Dubois, recommending the uneducated immigrant laborer for admission to the seminary, her prestige carried the day. Admitted in September 1820, Hughes graduated and was ordained a priest in 1826. His first assignment: the diocese of Philadelphia.

Recognized as a born leader from his early seminary days, he first came to prominence in Philadelphia as an eloquent and courageous crusader against bigotry. Between 1820 and 1830, immigration had swelled the U.S. Catholic population 60 percent to 600,000, with no end in sight. The new immigrants were mostly Irish—impoverished, ignorant, unskilled country folk, with nothing in their experience to prepare them for success in the urban environs to which they were flocking. Hughes believed that the relentless barrage of anti-Catholic prejudice that greeted them in their new land was demoralizing the already disadvantaged immigrants and holding back their progress.

The "nativists," as the highly organized anti-Catholics were called, included Protestant fundamentalists who saw the Catholic Church as the handiwork of Satan and superstition, intellectuals who considered Catholicism incompatible with democracy, ethnocentric cultural purists who believed the United States should be a land for Anglo-Saxons, and pragmatic citizens who thought it not worth the trouble to integrate so many culturally different immigrants. The nativists counted among their number many of America's elite, including John Jay, John Quincy Adams, John Calhoun, Stephen Douglas, and P. T. Barnum, all of whom spoke publicly against the Catholic Church and the threat to liberty that allowing Catholics into the country would create. In Boston a mob led by Congregationalist minister Lyman Beecher, the father of Harriet Beecher Stowe, burned a convent to the ground; church burnings were common. Samuel Morse tapped out rumors of Catholic conspiracies against liberty on his Atlantic cable long before such trash circulated on the Internet. Books depicting concupiscence in convents and sex in seminaries were everywhere.

Hughes was outraged. He didn't want Catholics to be second-class citizens in America as they had been in Ireland, and he thought he had a duty not to repeat the mistakes of the clergy in Ireland, who in his view had been remiss in not speaking out more forcefully against English oppression. Resistance was imperative. He began a letter-writing campaign to the newspapers, decrying what he saw as a tendency toward chauvinistic nationalism in his new country. In 1829, for instance, outraged by an editorial in a Protestant religious newspaper about "traitorous popery," he fired off a missive to its editorial board of Protestant ministers, calling them "the clerical scum of the Country." During the 1834 cholera epidemic in Philadelphia, which nativists blamed on Irish immigrants, Hughes worked tirelessly among the sick and dying, while many Protestant ministers fled the city to escape infection. After the disease subsided, Hughes wrote the *U.S. Gazette* that Protestant ministers were "remarkable for their pastoral solicitude, so long as the flock is healthy, the pastures pleasant, and the fleece lubricant, abandoning their post when disease begins to spread dissolution in the fold." He pointed to the work of the Catholic Sisters of Charity, who had cared for cholera victims without regard for their own safety, and wondered where all the people who spoke about perversion in the convents had gone during the epidemic.

The next year he became a national celebrity when a prominent and well-born Protestant clergyman from New York named John Breckenridge challenged him to a debate. The American aristocrat and the articulate, combative priest, who had developed a large following among Philadelphia's

7

Irish immigrants, did not disappoint their fans. Breckenridge luridly conjured up the Catholic Church's Inquisition in Spain, tyranny in Italy, and repression of liberty in France. Americans, he said, wanted no popery, no loss of individual liberty. Hughes countered by describing Protestant tyranny over Catholic Ireland. He related what had happened at his sister's grave. "I am an American by choice, not by chance," he said. "I was born under the scourge of Protestant persecution, of which my fathers in common with our Catholic countrymen have been the victim for ages. I know the value of that civil and religious liberty, which our happy government secures for all." Regardless of what had happened in Europe, he said, he was committed to American tolerance.

Hughes's performance against a man of Breckenridge's stature made him a hero with America's Irish. Not long thereafter, when John Dubois, Hughes's former teacher and now bishop of New York, grew sick and frail, Rome appointed Hughes, just over 40 years of age, coadjutor-bishop of the New York diocese, which then included all of New York State and part of New Jersey. He was consecrated a bishop in the old St. Patrick's Cathedral—still standing on Mott Street—on January 7, 1838. James Gordon Bennett, the famous Scottish-born editor and publisher of the *New York Herald*, was one of the rare souls among New York's 60,000 Catholics (out of a total population of 300,000) who weren't Irish. He harrumphed that Catholic rituals were pure poetry, especially episcopal consecrations, but to hold such a ceremony before the "general run of New York Irish was like putting gold rings through a pig's nose."

After the consecration, John Hughes was ready to lead. Unsystematic, disorganized, impulsively charitable, unable to keep his checkbook balanced, vain enough to wear a toupee over his baldness and combative enough to have to apologize to a valued colleague for "a certain pungency of style" in argument, Hughes was also, in the words of future president James Buchanan, "one of the ablest and most accomplished and energetic men I had ever known." Hughes's first New York crusade was to get his flock educated, so that they could benefit from the new nation's almost limitless opportunity. He passionately believed that the future of the Irish in America depended upon education: indeed, he knew it firsthand from his own experience.

He immediately stirred up a war over the city's schools, then run by the Public School Society. Though the society received state funding, it was essentially a private Protestant organization that taught Protestantism and used the Protestant Bible. Worse, from Hughes's point of view, it had pupils read such books as *The Irish Heart*, which taught that "the emigration from Ireland to America of annually increasing numbers, extremely needy, and in many cases drunken and depraved, has become a subject for all our grave and fearful reflection." Hughes (with the support of New York's twelve thousand Jews) wanted an end to such sectarian education, and he wanted, above all, state aid for Catholic schools, just as the state had funded denominational schools before 1826 (with no one dreaming of calling such aid unconstitutional). The outcome of the struggle pleased no one: the Maclay Bill of 1842 barred all religious instruction from public schools and provided no state money to denominational schools. On the night the bill was passed, a nativist mob ransacked Hughes's residence, and the authorities had to call out the militia to protect the city's Catholic churches.

Having at least partly reformed the public schools to help those Catholic children who attended them, Hughes threw his energies into building a Catholic school system that would educate Catholic children the way he thought they should be educated. No need was more urgent, in his view. He did not believe that a society hostile to the Irish and certain they were incapable of accomplishment would produce schoolteachers and administrators interested in and good at teaching Irish children. "We shall have to build the schoolhouse first and the church afterward," he said. "In our age the question of education is the question of the church."

Hughes's schools emphasized not just the three Rs but also a faith-based code of personal conduct that demanded respect for teachers and fellow students. Parents had to attend meetings with teachers and do repair work and cleaning in the schools. These schools then, as now, produced children capable of functioning in the mainstream of American life. By the end of his tenure, the original boundaries of Hughes's diocese contained over one hundred such schools. Not content to build just primary and secondary schools, he founded or helped to found Fordham University and Manhattan, Manhattanville, and Mount St. Vincent colleges.

In 1845 Hughes began to face his greatest challenge. That year the potato crop failed completely in Ireland, and the Great Famine struck, lasting until 1849. The worst famine in the history of Western Europe, it brought complete social collapse to Ireland and caused some two million Irish to flee to the United States between 1845 and 1860, not primarily for religious freedom and economic opportunity but to reach a place where they might eat. Most arrived at the port of New York after crossing the Atlantic on what they called "the coffin ships." As Thomas Sowell so vividly describes this journey in *Ethnic America*, the Irish packed into the holds of cargo ships, with no toilet facilities; filth and disease were rampant. They slept on narrow, closely stacked shelves. Women were so vulnerable to molestation that they slept sitting up. In 1847 about forty thousand died making the voyage, a mortality rate much higher than that of slaves transported from Africa in British vessels of the same period.

In New York they took up residence in homes intended for single families, which were subdivided into tiny apartments. Cellars became dwellings, as did attics three feet high, without sunlight or ventilation, where whole families slept in one bed. Shanties sprang up in alleys. Without running water, cleanliness was impossible; sewage piled up in backyard privies, and rats abounded. Cholera broke out constantly in Irish wards. Observers have noted that no Americans before or since have lived in worse conditions than the New York Irish of the mid-nineteenth century.

Hughes harbored no illusions about the newcomers. "Most move on across the country—those who have some means, those who have industrious habits," he observed; "on the other hand, the destitute, the disabled, the broken down, the very young, and the very old, having reached New York, stay. Those who stay are predominantly the scattered debris of the Irish nation." Lost in a land where many didn't want them, violent, without skills, the Irish were in need of rescue. This was Hughes's flock, and he was prepared to be their rescuer.

New York's Irish truly formed an underclass; every variety of social pathology flourished luxuriantly among them. Family life had disintegrated. Thomas D'Arcy McGee, an exiled Irish political radical, wrote in *The Nation* in 1850: "In Ireland every son was a boy and a daughter a girl till he or she was married. They were considered subjects to their parents till they became parents themselves. In America boys are men at sixteen. . . . If [the] family tie is snapped, our children become our opponents and sometimes our worst enemies." McGee saw that the lack of stable family relationships was fatally undermining the Irish community.

11

The immigrants crowded into neighborhoods like Sweeney's Shambles in the city's Fourth Ward and Five Points in the Sixth Ward (called the "Bloody Sixth" for its violence), which Charles Dickens toured in the forties and pronounced "loathsome, drooping, and decayed." In *The New York Irish*, Ronald Bayor and Timothy Meagher report that besides rampant alcoholism, addiction to opium and laudanum was epidemic in these neighborhoods in the 1840s and 1850s. Many Irish immigrants communicated in their own profanity-filled street slang called "flash talk": a multi-day drinking spree was "going on a bender"; "cracking a can" was robbing a house. Literate English practically disappeared from ordinary conversation.

An estimated fifty thousand Irish prostitutes, known in flash talk as "nymphs of the pave," worked the city in 1850, and Five Points alone had as many as seventeen brothels. Illegitimacy reached stratospheric heights—and tens of thousands of abandoned Irish kids roamed, or prowled, the city's streets. Violent Irish gangs, with names like the Forty Thieves, the B'boys, the Roach Guards, and the Chichesters, brought havoc to their neighborhoods. The gangs fought one another and the nativists—but primarily they robbed houses and small businesses, and trafficked in stolen property. Over half the people arrested in New York in the 1840s and 1850s were Irish, so that police vans were dubbed "paddy wagons" and episodes of mob violence in the streets were called "donnybrooks," after a town in Ireland.

Death was everywhere. In 1854 one out of every seventeen people in the Sixth Ward died. In Sweeney's Shambles the rate was one out of five in a twenty-two-month period. The death rate among Irish families in New York in the 1850s was 21 percent, while among non-Irish it was 3 percent. Life expectancy for New York's Irish averaged under forty years.

Tuberculosis, which Bishop Hughes called the "natural death of the Irish immigrants," was the leading cause of death, along with drink and violence.

Inflamed by this spectacle of social ruin, nativist sentiment grew and took a nastier, racist turn, no longer attacking primarily the superstition and priestcraft of the Catholic religion but rather the genetic inferiority of the Irish people. Gifted diarist and former mayor George Templeton Strong, for example, wrote that "the gorilla is superior to the Celtic in muscle and hardly their inferior in a moral sense." In the same vein, *Harper's* in 1851 described the "Celtic physiognomy" as "simian-like, with protruding teeth and short upturned noses." Celebrated cartoonist Thomas Nast constantly depicted the Irish as closely related to apes, while Orson and Lorenzo Fowler's *New Illustrated Self-Instructor in Phrenology* and James Redfield's *Outline of a New System of Physiognomy* gave such ideas the color of science.

By 1850 the New York City lunatic asylum on Blackwell's Island (now Roosevelt Island) was filled with Irish, most of them probably hallucinating alcoholics. Doctors of the day had a different view, speculating that insanity grew from degeneracy and violation of the moral law. Compounding the problem, according to Ralph Parsons, superintendent of the asylum, the Irish were people of exceptionally bad habits. They were, he said, of "a low order of intelligence, and very many of them have imperfectly developed brains. When such persons become insane, the prognosis is unfavorable."

Hughes's solution for his flock's social ills was to respiritualize them. He wanted to bring about an inner, moral transformation in them, which he believed would solve their social problems in the end. He put the ultimate blame for their condition squarely on the historical oppression they had suffered at the hands of the English, which he said had caused them "to pass away from the faith of their ancestors," robbing them of the cultural heritage that should have guided their behavior. But that was in the past: now it was time for them to regain what they had lost. So he bought abandoned Protestant church buildings in Irish wards, formed parish churches, and sent in parish priests on a mission of urban evangelization aimed at giving the immigrants a faith-based system of values.

With unerring psychological insight, Hughes had his priests emphasize religious teachings perfectly attuned to re-socializing the Irish and helping them succeed in their new lives. It was a religion of personal responsibility that they taught, stressing the importance of confession, a sacrament not widely popular today—and unknown to many of the Irish who emigrated during the famine, most of whom had never received any religious education. The practice had powerful psychological consequences. You cannot send a friend to confess for you, nor can you bring an advocate into the confessional. Once inside the confessional, you cannot discuss what others have done to you but must clearly state what you yourself have done wrong. It is the ultimate taking of responsibility for one's actions; and it taught the Irish to focus on their own role in creating their misfortune.

Hughes once remarked that "the Catholic Church is a church of discipline," and Father Richard Shaw, Hughes's most recent biographer, believes that the comment gives a glimpse into the inner core of his beliefs. Self-control and high personal standards were the key—and Hughes's own disciplined labors to improve himself and all those around him, despite constant ill health, embodied this ethic monumentally. Hughes proclaimed the need to avoid sin. His clergy stated clearly that certain conduct was right and other conduct was wrong. People must not govern their lives according to momentary feelings or the desire for instant gratification: they had to live up to a code of behavior that had been developed over thousands of years. This teaching produced communities where ethical standards mattered and severe stigma attached to those who misbehaved.

The priests stressed the virtue of purity, loudly and unambiguously, to both young and old. Sex was sinful outside marriage, no exceptions. Packed together in apartments with sometimes two or three families in a single room, the Irish lived in conditions that did not encourage chastity or even basic modesty. Women working in the low-paid drudgery of domestic service were tempted to work instead in the saloons of Five Points, which often led to a life of promiscuity or prostitution. The Church's fierce exhortations against promiscuity, with its accompanying evils of out-of-wedlock births and venereal disease, took hold. In time, most Irish began to understand that personal responsibility was an important component of sexual conduct.

Since alcohol was such a major problem for his flock, Hughes—though no teetotaler himself—promoted the formation of a Catholic abstinence society. In 1849 he accompanied the famous Irish Capuchin priest, Father Theobald Mathew, the "apostle of temperance," all around the city as he gave the abstinence pledge to twenty thousand New Yorkers.

A religion of discipline, stressing conduct and the avoidance of sin, can be a pinched and gloomy affair, but Hughes's teaching had a very different inflection. His priests mitigated the harshness with the encouraging Doctrine of the Sacred Heart, which declares that if you keep the commandments, God will be your protector, healer, advisor, and perfect personal friend. To a people despised by many, living in desperate circumstances, with narrow economic possibilities, such a teaching was a bulwark against anger, despair, and fear.

Hughes's Catholicism was upbeat and encouraging: if God Almighty was your personal friend, you could overcome.

Hughes's teaching had a special message for and about women. Women outnumbered men by 20 percent in New York's Irish population partly because of famine-induced emigration patterns and partly because many Irish immigrant men went west from New York to work on building railways and canals. Irish women could find work in New York more easily than men could, and the work they found, usually as domestics, was steadier. Given the demographic facts, along with the high illegitimacy rate and the degree of family disintegration, Hughes clearly saw the need to teach men respect for women, and women self-respect.

He did this by putting Catholicism's Marian Doctrine right at the center of his message. Irish women would hear from the priests and nuns that Mary was Queen of Peace, Queen of Prophets, and Queen of Heaven, and that women were important. The "ladies of New York," Hughes told them, were "the children, the daughters of Mary." The Marian teaching encouraged women to take responsibility for their own lives, to inspire their men and their children to good conduct, to keep their families together, and to become forces for upright behavior in their neighborhoods. The nuns, especially, encouraged women to become community leaders and play major roles in church fund-raising activities—radical notions for a male-dominated society where women did not yet have the right to vote. In addition, Irish men and women saw nuns in major executive positions, managing hospitals, schools, orphanages, and church societies—sending another highly unusual message for the day. Irish women became important allies in Hughes's war for values; by the 1850s they began to be major forces for moral rectitude, stability, and progress in the Irish neighborhoods of the city.

When Hughes went beyond spiritual uplift to the material and institutional needs of New York's Irish, he always focused sharply on self-help and mutual aid. On the simplest level, in all parishes he encouraged the formation of church societies—support groups, like today's women's groups or Alcoholics Anonymous, to help people deal with neighborhood concerns or personal and family problems, such as alcoholism or finding employment. In these groups, people at the local level could exchange information and advice, and offer one another encouragement and constructive criticism.

Hughes worked hard to get jobs for his flock. The nuns in his diocese became employment agencies for Irish domestics: rich families knew that a maid or cook recommended by the nuns would be honest and reliable. The nuns encouraged Irish women to run boarding houses for new immigrants and to become fruit and vegetable vendors. Irish women came to dominate the city's produce business, and some went on to succeed with their own grocery stores.

Hughes encouraged the formation of the Irish Emigrant Society, out of which the Emigrant Industrial Savings Bank later grew. The society helped find people jobs in sail making, construction, carriage repair and maintenance, and grocery stores. The society expected those it sponsored to behave properly on the job and work conscientiously, so as to reflect credit upon their patron. Those who misbehaved incurred the wrath not only of their employers but of the Emigrant Society and the parish priest, both unembarrassed about using shame to encourage good behavior.

When it came to charity, Hughes had nothing but contempt for the way New York officials went about it, warehousing the poor in the municipal almshouse and giving them subsistence levels of food, shelter, and clothing until they died, usually of typhus, typhoid fever, consumption, or cholera. Hughes dismissed this approach, which made no effort to remoralize the demoralized poor, as "soupery."

By contrast, Hughes imported church groups that had shown elsewhere in the world that they could help solve tough social problems. The most famous was the St. Vincent de Paul Society, a group of laymen who gave personal service to the poor. They visited prisons, organized youth groups, and taught reading and writing. Whenever they provided food, clothing, or shelter, they required the recipients, when possible, to work in return. An order of nuns, the Sisters of Mercy, worked closely with the St. Vincent de Paul Society, visiting the city's almshouses and prisons and urging the women in them to find work and to conduct themselves according to Church teachings. They founded their own home for immigrant girls, a halfway house between dependency and work, where they provided spiritual guidance, taught such basic skills as cooking and cleaning, and helped women find jobs, usually as domestics.

Faced with perhaps as many as sixty thousand Irish children wandering in packs around New York City—not attending school, not working, not under any adult supervision—Hughes encouraged the formation of the Society for the Protection of Destitute Catholic Children, known as the Catholic Protectory, which was in a sense the forerunner of Boys Town. To rescue these children, who in the words of the Protectory's head, Dr. Levi Silliman Ives, were "exposed to all the horrors of hopeless poverty, to the allurements of vice and crime in every disgusting and debasing form, bringing ruin on themselves and disgrace and obloquy," the Protectory purchased a 114-acre farm near Westchester and erected buildings for boys and girls. The mission was clear: the Protectory staff believed that, in Ives's words, "by proper religious instruction and the teaching of useful trades they could raise the children above their slum environment." Ives had no doubt that the children had to be taught sound values before they would have a chance at a productive life.

Though the Protectory received some city and state money, the Irish themselves provided its main support with enthusiastic private contributions. Hughes and Ives made it clear that these children were the community's responsibility: their own Irish parents—not the nativists or the unfeeling city—had abandoned them to their plight. The Irish, as Hughes and his priests and nuns tirelessly taught, had a moral responsibility to give money to this cause, as well as to the Church and all its other charitable organizations. For Hughes, such community self-help and personal responsibility were the essence of Christian charity.

By 1850 the city's Catholics had become so numerous that Rome made New York an archdiocese and Hughes an archbishop. He received the pallium, the woolen band that was the symbol of his new authority, directly from Pope Pius IX, a sign of the growing importance within the Church of American Catholics in general, of New York's Catholics in particular, and of Hughes himself. As the 1850s wore on, the archbishop began to conceive a plan that would give magnificent, concrete expression to the rise of New York's Catholics. He would build a great cathedral, financed by the Catholics themselves, as proof to the Protestant elites that the Irish, too, knew how to make New York the premier city of the world. More important, such an accomplishment would give an enormous boost to the morale of the Irish community itself—which, however poor, was not too poor to achieve something grand.

Hughes laid the cornerstone on August 15, 1858, before a crowd of over 100,000, their imaginations fired by the hugely ambitious project. He had raised only $73,000 of the project's estimated $1.5 million cost (a figure that ultimately rose to over $4 million, a staggering sum for the nineteenth century). But Hughes believed that if you took on a challenge, you

19

would perforce rise to meet it. St. Patrick's was finished in 1879 by his successor, John McCloskey, who raised the final $172,000 by holding a giant fair in the nave of the new cathedral for 42 days.

In 1863, with construction of the cathedral suspended because of the Civil War, the worst urban rioting in United States history broke out among the Irish in New York. Over one thousand people were killed in three days. The Irish were enraged that the Union army was drafting them in disproportionate numbers because they could not afford the then-legal practice of buying their way out of military service. Irish boys, who made up about 15 percent of the Union army, were suffering horrific casualty rates since they were commonly used as frontline troops against better-trained and better-led Confederate soldiers. In addition, rumors spread that once the slaves were freed, they would take Irish jobs or live off taxes on the Irish. The rioting Irish attacked blacks, nativists, and, on the third day, anybody who was around.

A then-dying Archbishop Hughes summoned the leaders of the rebellion to meet with him. However disturbed he might have been that the Irish were being called on to do so much of the dying in the struggle against the South, he supported the war and was totally opposed to slavery, having preached against it since his ordination as a priest in 1826. He told the riot leaders that "no blood of innocent martyrs, shed by Irish Catholics, has ever stained the soil of Ireland" and that they were dishonoring that impeccable history.

The riot leaders went back to their neighborhoods, and the violence melted away. The riot saddened the dying archbishop: he felt he had failed as a prelate. His friend and loyal subordinate, Bishop McCloskey, was saying the prayers for the dying when the end came for Hughes on January 3, 1864.

He had not failed, of course. The Draft Riots of 1863 were

the death rattle of a destructive culture that was giving way to something constructive and edifying.

Though just thirty or forty years before, New Yorkers had viewed the Irish as their criminal class, by the 1880s and 1890s the Irish proportion of arrests for violent crime had dropped from 60 percent to less than 10 percent. The Irish were the pillars of the criminal justice system. Three-quarters of the police force was Irish. The Irish were the prosecutors, the judges, and the jailers.

Alcoholism and drug addiction withered away. By the 1880s an estimated 60 percent of Irish women, and almost a third of the men, totally abstained from alcohol. Many Irish sections in the city became known for their peacefulness, order, and cleanliness—a far cry from the filth, violence, and disease of the Five Points and Sweeney's Shambles of mid-century. Gone, too, was the notorious Irish promiscuity of those years; New York's Irish became known by the latter part of the nineteenth century as a churched people, often chided by the press for their "puritanical" attitudes. Irish prostitutes virtually disappeared in the city, as did the army of Irish youths wandering the streets without adult supervision. Irish family life, formerly so frayed and chaotic, became strong and nourishing. Irish children entered the priesthood or the convent, the professions, politics, professional sports, show business, and commerce. In 1890 some 30 percent of New York City's teachers were Irish women, and the Irish literacy rate exceeded 90 percent. In 1871 reformer "Honest" John Kelly became the leader of Tammany Hall, and with the election in 1880 of shipping magnate William Grace as mayor, the Irish assumed control of city politics.

How important a figure was John Hughes in American history? Suppose the mass immigration from Ireland of the mid-nineteenth century had turned into a disaster for the country. How likely is it that the open immigration of the late nineteenth and early twentieth centuries would have been permitted? Nativism would have won, and America would be an unrecognizably different country today—and an immeasurably poorer one.

[1997]

WILLIAM J. STERN

Once We Knew How to Rescue Poor Kids

THOSE WHO CARE about the fate of the underclass can learn much from the experience of New York's Irish in the second half of the nineteenth century. The nation's first underclass—criminal, drunken, promiscuous, and shiftless, with high illegitimacy rates and thousands of abandoned children—the Irish had so dramatically improved themselves as to enter the American mainstream triumphantly by the turn of the century. The Catholic Church, rather than any government effort, was the main agent of their reclamation, and no Catholic institution shows more clearly just how that transformation was achieved than New York's Society for the Protection of Destitute Catholic Children, which most called the Catholic Protectory. In June 1893, thirty years after the Protectory took in its first wayward child, a national conference on charity took the measure of its success. "What crimes have been prevented," the conference report declared, "what homes have been made happy, what human misery has been alleviated, what brands have been salvaged from the burning, what myriads of useful men and women have been made an honor to the state by this institution, it is beyond the power of the human pen to record."

The Protectory was the creation of a remarkable New Yorker by adoption named Dr. Levi Silliman Ives, whom no one could have foreseen would have fathered such a creation. But in hindsight, it's clear that several strands in his personal history went straight into the making of the Protectory.

First was Ives's own early poverty. Born a Connecticut Yankee in 1797 into a Presbyterian family whose ancestor had come ashore in Massachusetts Bay in 1635, he grew up dirt-poor in a bark shelter in West Turin, New York, where his failed-businessman father had moved the family. Ives, his parents, and some of his nine younger siblings worked as ill-paid hired hands in a sawmill. Perhaps the poverty grated all the more on Ives because his parents were related to a constellation of prosperous and well-known New England families; indeed, his Revolutionary War–hero uncle, down the road in West Turin, was a well-off farmer.

When Ives was fifteen, he enlisted in the War of 1812, in keeping with a family history of fierce American patriotism. After the war, he enrolled at Hamilton College in Clinton, New York, but in his third year, felled by a serious respiratory illness, he dropped out. In 1815, while he was still at Hamilton, his father, "melancholy from want of prosperity," according to a contemporary, drowned himself (though one wonders whether the melancholy was the effect or the cause of the penury). Poverty, war, illness, a father's failure and suicide—

these were Ives's tumultuous formative experiences. After he left West Turin, escaping his past, he had no further contact with his family and never mentioned them in his published writings or even in his surviving correspondence.

Ives's interest in religion kindled as he convalesced from illness; he soon took the first step in what would prove a long, restless spiritual quest. In this quest is visible the second of those character traits that led to the Protectory: the implacable intellectual honesty that led him to look closely at all available evidence and follow it to whatever conclusion it led.

While still in his teens, he took over a Presbyterian academy in Potsdam, New York, and gained a reputation as an electrifying revivalist preacher. But he had growing doubts about Presbyterianism, and, when he discovered the beauty of the Episcopal *Book of Common Prayer* and the writings of Episcopal bishop John Henry Hobart, rector of New York City's Trinity Church—America's biggest and richest parish—he wrote to him, confiding his doubts and asking for information about the Episcopal faith. The bishop invited him to New York, and, soon after, Ives entered Hobart's General Theological Seminary at Chelsea Square. Upon graduation in 1822, Ives became an Episcopal deacon and served in upstate New York and in Philadelphia. At the same time, he was courting Bishop Hobart's daughter, Rebecca, whom he married in 1825 and to whom he remained devoted his entire life. Two years later, he became rector of Saint Luke's Church in Greenwich Village, then still virtually suburban—and a long way from the bark shelter in West Turin. The congregation doubled during Ives's tenure and he turned down offers from bigger, more established parishes.

Tall, handsome, dedicated, and cerebral—a "practical ascetic," as his biographer John O'Grady rightly calls him—Ives was clearly a man on the rise in what was the religion of the

American elites. In 1831, rising still further, he became Episcopal bishop of North Carolina.

It was among the destitute of that southern state that the
last two personal qualities that bore fruit in the Protectory first
blossomed: Ives's devotion to the poor and his talents as an
institution builder. More missionary than theologian, he believed that to be truly Christian, one had to work directly with
the poor—it was, he wrote, "what a man must do to be
saved."

With its illness-breeding climate, North Carolina was a
coarse and brutal place: public hangings provided a major
source of popular entertainment. Among the state's illiterate,
impoverished, and declining population, Ives found plenty of
the poor to help. His chief rescue strategy was to found
schools, as he would later do in founding the Protectory. In
Raleigh, he established a school dedicated to providing faith-
based values and a rigorous education to one hundred or so
students, most of them poor and ignorant boarders no older
than fourteen—one of whom had traveled a month on horse-
back to attend the school from the banks of the Yazoo River in
Mississippi. Educationally, the school was a great success, but
financially, though its classes were filled to brimming, it
failed, when the national economic crisis of 1837 dried up its
funding. Even more ambitiously, with $400—much of it from
New York friends—Ives bought an entire valley in the moun-
tainous western part of North Carolina and set up a missionary school called Valle Crucis, modeled after an early
Christian monastery and aimed at the poorest of the state's
poor. But the money was too scant, and the wild mountain
boys too unruly: this school failed, too. Ives learned from the
failures that good intentions weren't sufficient for an institution to survive. You also had to pay attention to practical matters, such as raising money.

Ives's solicitude for the downtrodden extended to North Carolina's slaves. He was no abolitionist, but he worked to bring the Gospel both to slaves and to free blacks. He composed a catechism to use in teaching slaves, and he openly defended two plantation owners who had hired a full-time chaplain to teach their slaves religion. He encouraged plantation owners to treat their slaves well and to worship with them, believing that, as Christianity changed the culture over time, slavery might wither away. One scholar, Michael Taylor, sums up Ives's attitude thus: help individual slaves, but say nothing about the institution of slavery. We might gloss it differently: like the founder of Christianity, Ives left political revolution to others. The revolution that interested him was in the mind and heart.

While Ives pursued his philanthropic projects in North Carolina, his questing intellectual spirit was working deep, as yet subterranean, changes in his religious life. As he had risen in the Episcopal hierarchy, the Oxford Movement within the Anglican Church had taken fire in England, and it included some of the most brilliant minds in England—most notably, of course, John Henry Newman, who, like several other prominent members, later converted to Catholicism. The movement looked to the early Christian experience to grasp the true meaning of Christianity, which included, the Oxford writers believed, a strong emphasis on pastoral and charitable work. (The movement formulated the twelve-step program that Alcoholics Anonymous and almost all addiction treatment groups use today.) Bishop Hobart had introduced Ives to the Oxford Movement as early as the mid-1820s. Its influence had grown within Ives as he ministered to the poor in North Carolina, and it began to lead him, waveringly though inexorably, down Newman's path to Rome.

As he later explained in his spiritual autobiography, a

27

strangely withholding memoir that gives little real insight into the man's private self, the Episcopal Church he knew didn't answer for him the overwhelming need—if one were truly to be Christian—to walk with the poor. "Your churches and houses, and sympathies and charities," Ives wrote, stating the Gospel message as he understood it, "will be thrown widely open to them." But in the Episcopal Church of his time, Ives felt he "could see nothing which marked it as the hope and the home of the wretched; nothing which proclaimed its peculiar fellowship with the poor." Episcopal houses of worship, Ives thought, excluded the poor: "The very arrangement said aloud to the rich, 'sit thou here in a good place'; and to the poor, 'stand thou there, or sit here under my footstool.'" For Ives, who had known the humiliation of poverty, the Catholic Church satisfied his calling to help the destitute.

But imagine the painful dilemma he faced. Though conversion, he became convinced, offered him "peace of conscience, and the salvation of my soul," he later wrote, the idea of it filled him with "horror, . . . enhanced by the self-humiliation with which I saw such a step must cover me, the absolute deprivation of all mere temporal support which it must occasion, not only to myself, but to one whom I was bound 'to love and cherish until death.'" Ives indeed stood to lose the considerable worldly honor and eminence he had attained within the Episcopal Church. And Ives was right: what would it do to his wife? Her life had not been easy after she married him. The Iveses had lost both their young children to illness, a crushing blow. Rebecca Ives was frequently ill herself. She found the harshness of North Carolina and the distance from her family in New York hard to endure. And her father—Ives's great, almost fatherly, benefactor—was before his death in 1828 the very embodiment of American Episcopalianism. If Ives converted, wouldn't it betray Bishop Hobart's memory and force Rebecca to choose painfully between her husband and her late father?

But Ives always was faithful to the truth as he saw it—in all ways—however much pain and personal cost this might entail. Tormented, the fifty-five-year-old cleric traveled to Rome in 1852 and became the first Protestant bishop since the Reformation to convert to Catholicism. Signaling Ives's prominence, it was Pope Pius IX who confirmed him into the Church the day after Christmas in 1852. A firestorm of controversy ensued, with the Protestant press and establishment denouncing Ives as mentally ill and bereft of integrity, and the Catholic press responding with a bizarre triumphalism, as though the Church had just won a high-profile sporting event. Ives's own brother came out against him and spoke, perhaps with their father's suicide in mind, of a family history of insanity.

When Ives returned from Rome in 1854, he settled in New York, which he had left twenty-three years earlier. No longer an exalted Episcopal bishop but now an ordinary Catholic layman, he would find his role ministering not to the city's elite, as he had from the pulpit of Saint Luke's, but to its most down-and-out denizens. The extraordinary archbishop of New York, "Dagger" John Hughes, ignoring the controversy that swirled around Ives, saw an imposing, learned man whose many talents he could use to help the Church. (See "How Dagger John Saved New York's Irish.") Hughes at once put Ives to work teaching at Saint Joseph's Seminary, at the Convent of the Sacred Heart in Manhattanville, and at the Academy of Mount Saint Vincent in Westchester.

Hughes knew Ives would be an asset to the Church as an educator but soon learned that he would play an even more crucial role in the Church's charitable mission. Ives immediately joined the St. Vincent de Paul Society in Manhattanville and quickly became its New York leader. Formed in Paris during the 1830s as a Catholic response to socialist anticlericalism, class hatred, and political radicalism, the society took as its motto: go to the poor. It buried the dead, brought food, provided shelter, taught Sunday school, counseled alcoholics and troubled families, and cared for orphans, among many other intense, face-to-face ministrations to the poor.

New York City—and its Catholic Church—had no more pressing concern in the 1850s than to figure out what to do about the more than sixty thousand abandoned, mostly illegitimate, Irish kids who roved the city in gangs with scary names like the Forty Thieves, the B'boys, and the Roach Guards, and terrorized citizens day and night. Thomas D'Arcy McGee, a tough Irish political exile, wanted to drum up opposition to the English among the New York Irish; instead, he found himself more frightened of Irish teen thugs in New York City than he was of English soldiers in Ireland. Ives was acutely aware of the depraved condition of the Irish kids. Never, he remarked, had he witnessed "a more utter disregard of honor, of truth and purity and even the common decencies of life."

Where did they come from? For Archbishop Hughes, whose views Ives shared, they were the products of Irish family breakdown—a reminder that today's underclass had a precursor with remarkably similar traits. Trying to figure out how to save the children of this broken community, Ives began to study how various charities actually worked. He was a model social scientist, for—just as in his religious quest—he let the data lead him to the truth instead of conforming it to a predisposed vision.

Nothing seemed to work, he soon discovered. If the failed policies seem familiar, it's because the modern social services industry still trots them out. One idea was to change the kids' environment and give them jobs. The government sent wild

30

Irish city kids to midwestern farms, assuming that Calvinist hard work—and maybe the fresh air—would reform them. Ives knew it was bunk: "[I]f you take a vicious child from the streets of the city and send him to the farms," he observed, "what you get is a vicious farm worker." After all, taking a kid out of the slums isn't really changing his environment, as partisans of the farmwork solution believed; the environment that really counts for delinquent kids, Ives understood, is in their minds and hearts.

The government also tried the foster-home solution. The St. Vincent de Paul Society did this, too, so Ives saw how it worked up close. Over time, he grew skeptical. "I had been in the practice of securing good homes for untrained and destitute Catholic children," he later said, "and although I succeeded in finding places for many, I can call to mind only a single instance where the child did not either abscond or prove ungovernable and worthless." Since these kids were largely unsocialized—no one had ever imposed structure on their lives, taught them moral values, or shown them love— they tended to be too much to handle even for the most well-intentioned family. As psychiatrist George Hogben puts it, "Most functioning families will not be willing to establish the intense psychological structure and rigid discipline such children require."

As Ives continued to search for an answer, he learned about the innovative charitable efforts of two East-Coast priests. Father George Haskins—like Ives, a former Episcopalian—ran a Catholic school in Boston that gave two years of intensive religious instruction to boys whom today we'd call "at risk." Haskins's school, Ives saw, had clearly improved the boys' behavior. In Baltimore, Father James Dolan tried something different. He stressed vocational training, but kept the boys in his home until they could support themselves. Here, too, Ives saw an improvement in the boys as they learned new skills. But both initiatives weren't by themselves enough, Ives believed. They needed to be combined.

Accordingly, Ives brought the Protectory into being, securing its charter from the State Legislature on April 14, 1863, and being elected president a few weeks later by an almost entirely Irish board of directors. The institution opened its doors in May 1863, in small rented quarters in two buildings on East 36th and 37th Streets. At first restricted to boys, the Protectory started its girls' division a few months later at the corner of 8th Street and Second Avenue. A little later, needing more room, the Protectory moved all its charges to two big rented buildings on 86th Street, near Fifth Avenue. The Christian Brothers, a lay group devoted to education, ran the boys' division; the Sisters of Charity, a religious order that looked after the sick and the destitute, took charge of the girls. In 1870, after Ives's death, the Protectory moved to a 114-acre site in Parkchester—then part of Westchester but now incorporated into the Bronx—that Ives had purchased in 1865. It operated there until it closed permanently in November 1938, when the city no longer had enough Catholic delinquents to fill it. Over the years, it sheltered more than 100,000 children, two-thirds of them boys.

In the Protectory's first annual report, Ives explained how it differed from other charities. It wanted to do something more for its charges, Ives suggested, "than merely rid the city of them, at great expense, for a few months, to return . . . or to become to some other place a more grievous charge than when they left." Instead, it sought to raise them from a state of "indolence, stupidity and vice" to one in which they would "acknowledge their obligation to God, to their parents and to society." It would "raise them from their state of degradation and misery and . . . place them in a condition in which they have a fair chance to work out for themselves a better destiny." Ives sought, in short, to re-socialize young ruffians. "Our great aim," he stressed, "is to mould their hearts to the practice of virtue, and while we make them worthy citizens of our glorious Republic, to render them fit candidates for the heavenly mansions above." He had his work cut out for him: because of tight financial realities, he could only take in kids the courts handed over, since he would get additional public funds for them—about $120 per kid per year of the roughly $350 per-kid cost. Thus, Ives had mostly juvenile delinquents—the roughest Irish youth—under the Protectory's wing.

The key to re-socializing the children, Ives believed, lay in giving them a faith-based system of values. "Every child committed to this institution," he proclaimed, "will be thoroughly trained in the faith and morality of the Gospel as revealed and entrusted to the Catholic Church." On first sight, this might look like boilerplate, without much meaning except to believers. But recall that religion has a centuries-old experience in effectively teaching people the difference between right and wrong, and that some of the most up-to-date social thinkers have rediscovered inner-city ministries as one of the most effective agencies for redeeming underclass kids today. It's easy enough to understand what these ministers are doing, and why Ives was successful, in modern, purely psychological terms. The Protectory provided the clearest possible statement of right and wrong, confidently asserted that these values were absolute and backed up by divine authority, provided a discipline of practice and reflection that reinforced these values, held out complete forgiveness for past wrongdoing, and offered membership in a community organized around this code. Speaking more broadly still, Ives understood that at the center of the underclass condition is a moral and social void, and he knew how to fill it.

Respect was an essential component of the Protectory's moral lesson—respect for oneself, for parents, for other children, for teachers, and for God. Ives wanted to introduce the children to a world of obligations and make them aware that they weren't the sole arbiters of what they should and shouldn't do. He cultivated in them a host of ethical responsibilities where formerly there had been only caprice and impulse. Among other things, he made the Protectory children responsible for one another. "[I]t has occurred several times that a couple of our boys, having been sent on an errand to the city, have there fallen in with one who absconded, and have brought him back in triumph to the Protectory," Ives proudly observed.

One of the most effective disciplines the Protectory used to turn impulsive, often criminally inclined, children into personally responsible individuals was the sacrament of confession. Confession meant that each week the children had to examine their behavior, decide if it conformed to the ethical code they'd been taught, and take responsibility for it by confessing to a priest. Thus, they learned to reflect habitually on themselves and on morality, to lead an examined and responsible life.

The Protectory's Catholic teaching gave more than a stern set of dos and don'ts to these emotionally shipwrecked children. It offered them love and a sense of their own worthiness. If you keep the commandments, Ives's teachers told the children, God would be father and friend, offering an infinite and unshakable love. For children who had never known a parent's tender care, this was strong solace. The sacrament of the Eucharist had an equally positive psychological resonance for Protectory dependents, dramatizing to them that an all-powerful God had been willing to sacrifice his own son for their sake—that's how much they were worth. This teaching conveyed a powerful message of self-esteem, to use today's debased term.

Ives aimed to give the Protectory's children the means of making a living. He "resolved to cause these children . . . to be trained in some industrial occupation or mechanic art while they are instructed in all the essential branches of an English education." Vocational training also had a moral purpose, Ives believed, for it "diverts young minds from the evil suggestions of the tempter." "In the workshop," he added, "we have found the most direct and effectual corrective for an idle, vicious boy." As early as 1868, the Protectory had trained 185 boys as shoemakers, 45 as gardeners, and a half-dozen as bakers; 56 girls had learned how to make dresses. Twenty years later the Protectory had added stereotyping, blacksmithing, carpentry, tailoring, and other trades to its curriculum. By the turn of the century, the Protectory even trained many of its charges in electrical engineering, masonry, and plumbing. Ives was not turning out ditchdiggers.

Ives believed that classical and sacred music were crucial to a complete education. He launched a full brass band and a string orchestra at the Protectory. Playing in a band or orchestra taught kids how to play their parts exactly in a disciplined communal activity to which they were essential. Beyond that, the message of serious music is order, harmony, and transcendence, all in tune with the Protectory's teachings.

The inner and outer worlds of abandoned children are chaotic—to them, frighteningly so—and Ives understood those kids' special need for rigid structure, to provide them with a sense that the world is secure and predictable and to bring some order to their emotional lives. Everything at the

35

Protectory took place according to an almost military schedule, providing the all-encompassing, minute-by-minute structure whose lack, as Ives perhaps intuited, is the reason even good foster care so often fails. The weekday began at 5:30 and provided slots for chapel and prayer, for meals, for classes and study periods, for shopwork or groundskeeping, for recess and even a little evening recreation time, and for lots of regimented, military-style drill for the boys and highly structured group dance routines for the girls. During the weekend, the kids had religious instruction and music. These wayward children, who once had time hanging heavy on their hands, now used almost every waking minute for self-improvement.

In sum, Ives sought a total inner transformation of the Protectory's wards. He wanted to educate them, give them useful skills, and, most of all, change their values and worldview. A practical man, he wasn't preparing children for the monastic life; he wanted them to be "worthy, influential and prosperous" in an America he described as "unsettled and money making"—not a bad description of present-day America. He wanted to instill in them the hope that, through hard work, they might support themselves and a family and even become wealthy.

Did Ives succeed? Did his Irish charges become self-reliant? According to historian George Paul Jacoby, the answer is an unambiguous yes. Boys found jobs when they left the Protectory, and, Jacoby observes, "many soon became very prosperous in the trades for which they were trained." In the single year of 1876, Jacoby records, the Protectory found positions for 186 children throughout New York, and in almost every case, "the result was gratifying." Some of the kids even went on to study the classics at university—a remarkable fact, given that the vast majority of them were more or less illiterate when they first came to the Protectory.

Outsiders who evaluated the Protectory were warm in their approval. In 1878, Elisha H. Harris of the U.S. Health Department praised the institution for cultivating in the children "obedience, order, cleanliness, and diligence," and, above all, "a reverence for their Creator and his divine behests." An 1893 National Conference on Charity and Correction viewed the Protectory as a model philanthropic enterprise: "He who visits the Protectory on one of its holidays, notes the many gymnastic exercises or the splendid military drill through which the boys are put; their graceful delivery in the recitation of pieces; the sweet songs they sing, and the superb band of 75 pieces that discourses music more like professionals than amateurs; observes the boys in the baseball field; looks into the work done by boys and girls in the classroom; or he who visits the workshops of the boys, and the serving-rooms of the girls, when in full operation, notes the industry and taste with which they perform their various duties—such a one can form some conception of the good that is accomplished by both departments of this institution." The conference pointed to other evidence in making its case, including enthusiastic endorsements from philanthropist William F. Barnard of the Five Points House of Industry in 1878 and from a state committee on the causes of crime in 1882.

Another testament to the Protectory's success is the quality of the goods its workshops produced. The Protectory's shoes, dresses, and other products drew high praise, even from across the ocean. Leading London papers, including the *Times*, the *Standard*, and the *Globe*, as well as Dublin's *Freeman*, dispensed such praise as: "The women's shoes are of the very neatest, most finely finished, and of the best make," or "the handiwork shown is of a remarkably high order," or yet again, "these specimens of work are really startling, and go to show what may be done with the classes of youth which in earlier

37

years have had but few, if any, opportunities for development or self-help." Skilled craftsmen are rare and the product of much cultivation, and to get such high-quality work—the kind of work that mobilizes so many human potentialities—from this human material is a sure sign that Ives's grand project was doing something profoundly right.

Additional evidence for the Protectory's success comes from the often moving testimonies from former charges that appear in the *Protectory News*, a literate and chatty newsletter the institution began to publish in 1910. One issue from the World War I period closed with a story of a former pupil, Edward Farley, now a soldier, who had promised his devout mother that he would wear a ribbon on his arm until he had stained his soul with mortal sin. As he lay dying from wounds received in battle, Farley told the chaplain attending to him to make sure his mother knew that he had worn the ribbon right up to the moment he died.

A 1910 issue of the *News* offered this success story: "After 44 years," wrote Peter M. Gillen, "I can never forget you and your kindness to me and your untiring efforts to instill in me the necessary education. I became . . . a first-class book and newspaper compositor and for more than 20 years held the post of proof reader on the *World*, *Herald*, and *Tribune*. I have been married 34 years, having had 12 children. . . . Two of my children are musicians (pianists) in great demand and who earn good money."

The editor praises another letter, from Archie Reilly, for its absence of all "etymological and syntactical errors." Reilly writes: "Mr. Deery is a very nice gentleman and is affording me every opportunity of learning the business of wholesale Quarry agents. I am also studying shorthand and am quite sure I shall succeed in learning it thoroughly. I find myself getting along nicely and have splendid hopes that with the blessing of God, perseverance and an abundance of energy, I may have a bright future." Reilly couldn't have offered a more fitting restatement of Ives's hopes in founding the Catholic Protectory.

Ives's influence spread. In Baltimore, Archbishop Spalding modeled the Saint Mary's Industrial School after the Protectory, and schools soon opened in California, Illinois, Kentucky, and Missouri that looked to it as a major influence. Parochial schools nationwide embraced Ives's approach, and Ives himself traveled the country evangelizing for his ideas on charity. In his last years, which he spent at Saint Joseph's Cottage on 138th Street near Broadway, Ives received a multitude of visitors from across the country, who sought his advice on how to establish and run charitable organizations. He died on October 14, 1867, just after his friends lifted up his head so that he could look one last time at Domenichino's sublime painting *The Last Communion of Saint Jerome*. Fittingly, he was buried on the grounds of the Catholic Protectory. The poet John Savage summed up Ives's dedication to New York's Irish poor: "His tender sympathies, and the necessities so sadly prominent in a great city, naturally led him to good works."

His example sheds light on the quiet struggle that has recently broken out for the soul of Catholic Charities, the $2.25 billion social services behemoth of which Ives was a founder. On one side, the organization's leadership echoes the social services industry's party line. Typical is the complaint of president Fred Kammer, a Jesuit, that the welfare-reform debate a couple of years ago had "focused almost exclusively on personal responsibility" and had ignored "the right to suitable employment and just and adequate wages." On the other side, critics like Senator Rick Santorum object that, if Catholic Charities is "only going to be a more efficient bureaucracy, if [it is] not going to feed the souls as well as the stomach, then why

39

exist?" Santorum and his allies reflect the guiding spirit Ives brought to Catholic Charities a century ago. The fact that Ives's approach worked so well powerfully argues in favor of the Santorum point of view.

Today, as Catholic Charities USA—the central office—pursues the expansion of the welfare state, there's less and less religion in its mission and less and less understanding of Ives's central insight that for charity to succeed, it must change the cultural attitudes of its recipients. It's a pity, since the welfare state can't solve the social problems—from illegitimacy to drug addiction—that we face at the end of the twentieth century. Certainly, Catholic Charities would be immeasurably more a force for good if it rediscovered the wisdom of Levi Silliman Ives. And our entire national effort to help the underclass would benefit immeasurably from reflecting on his example of changing the inner culture of the poor, too.

[1998]

HOWARD HUSOCK

How the Agency
Saved My Father

THE BIGGEST MYSTERY of my childhood was the question of
how my father had survived his. Though the details were
fuzzy, the facts seemed clear: an auto accident outside Trenton, in which his parents were seriously injured; orphaned,
not long after, in South Philadelphia in the depth of the Depression, ultimately raised in foster homes . . . and yet, by
eighteen, off by streetcar to engineering school and, after the
war, to life in the middle class.

What had made it possible? The most intriguing explanation involved something he called the Agency. "Once a year,"
he would say, "the Agency took us to get a suit—one pair of
long pants, one pair of knickers." Or: "The Agency even paid
to get my teeth fixed—before antibiotics, so you had to go
once a week to get the root canal drained so it wouldn't get in-

41

fected." Or: "Even though it was the Depression and everyone was poor, my sister would insist on getting off the streetcar a block away from the Agency, so when we went to see the doctor no one would know we were getting charity."

In a thousand ways, the world of my father's childhood amid the row houses of South Philly—a world where fish were kept alive in the bathtub so they'd stay fresh, where teenagers enjoyed classical music, where sunflower seeds were the junk food of choice—is as gone as any European *shtetl*. But to me, the Agency was the most distant part of it: my own father, it appeared, had been raised without parents and without the support of public funds, under the auspices of a charitable organization. Though recent talk about how "faith-based charity" should have a role in "social-service delivery" has made my father's experience seem a little less outlandish, the mystery haunted me. I wanted to solve it, both as a personal matter and a policy one. What exactly was the Agency? How did it compare with its successors? And—here's the personal part of the query—what effects of its work have I, unknowingly, lived with myself?

My father provided the crucial clue. Once a month, he recalled, an older woman, connected with the Agency, would arrive in a chauffeur-driven black Cadillac to check on him. Her name: Mrs. Sternberger.

I found her traces a few blocks from Independence Hall, at the Balch Institute for Ethnic Studies, which houses the records of Philadelphia's myriad Jewish charities. On the founding board of directors of the Juvenile Aid Society, I discovered, was a woman named Matilda K. Sternberger. And looking through the Juvenile Aid Society's pile of typed case records, I turned up the March 2, 1934, proceedings of its Placement Committee's monthly meeting—which took up the case of Bernard Husock and his elder sister Sylvia.

It is a powerful thing to come across such a record only

minutes before library closing time. It is sobering to read about one's own family as the object of intervention and help—especially when you're used to identifying with those providing the help, and even more especially when such records contain powerful revelations, as these did. I learned that my father's parents had not died at the same time; his father had outlived his mother and become a single father, responsible for two young children, aged five and ten, in the early years of the depression. I learned that in June 1932, three years before the Social Security Act became law, at a time when state and local governments provided only short-term emergency relief, my grandfather had first turned to private charity for support. So my father and his sister were not, as I had believed, simple examples of orphans cared for by charity. Their situation was more like that so common today: a single-parent family in search of help, a family for which outsiders were deciding whether help was deserved and, if so, what form that help should take.

By the time it considered the case of my father, the Juvenile Aid Society had been making such decisions for more than twenty years. It grew out of the Young Women's Union, which was part of a movement, beginning in the 1880s, in which (as Philadelphia's *Jewish Exponent* later wrote) "the noxious tenements of South Philadelphia were invaded by an unlikely little army of well-bred, carefully nurtured Jewish young ladies from the safely upper-middle-class environs of Spring Garden Street." Led by banking heiress Bella Loeb Selig, the union began to move from children's recreation and nursery programs to an effort its members called "baby snatching"—by which they meant persuading the Juvenile Court (founded in 1901) to release children in trouble into their custody. To handle these kids, the union gave birth to the Juvenile Aid Society in 1911.

By 1932, it was a big organization, paying for the care of

350 children in any given week (rising to 450 in the high-immigration early 1920s) with an annual budget of $100,000, almost all raised from private donations. It was part of a larger system of some eighty private nonprofit and religious organizations, which cared for the vast majority of abused, abandoned, or orphaned children in Pennsylvania—many more than the 600 or so children housed in five state institutions at a cost of around $150,000 a year.

Through the Juvenile Aid Society, the wealthy German-Jewish women on its board expressed their sense of responsibility for the children of poor "Russian" immigrants, their generic term for Eastern European Jews. So it was that women named Deutsch and Guckenheimer—members, many of them, of the city's grand Moroccan-style Reform temple, Congregation Rodeph Shalom—came to take some responsibility for children named Lazarowitz and Katz, then piling into South Philadelphia and crowding it with what ultimately would be more than two hundred small, dark synagogues, squeezed in among the row houses.

These charitable women can be thought of as Jewish Victorians, combining a religious impulse with the Victorian commitment to "child saving." They were moved by the Talmudic injunction that "the blessed man is the man that brings up an orphan boy or girl until marriage has given him another home," and—fearing that the Russians would abandon Judaism as they acculturated to America—they required all children they assisted to attend religious schools, known formally as Jewish Education Centers. For them, religion was the guarantor of the bourgeois values and the self-discipline they cherished. "Moral behavior," the Agency's literature observes, "is the result of right habit and daily practice. . . . Cultivate the child's natural desires for leadership, for justice, for independence, for self-respect, for hero-worship. Morality is an inner driving force. Religion is an inner light and revelation. These cannot be forced from without. Open the windows of the soul through which the inner splendor may shine."

Their religion was a far cry from the religious-sounding goal of so much Jewish philanthropy today—the notion, drawn from the Protestant social gospel, that religion has a duty to set right the injustices of society. These women would have met with incredulity the pronouncements of today's influential "child protection" advocates, who assert (in the words of Peter Pecora, James Whittaker, and Anthony Maluccio's standard *The Child Welfare Challenge*) that "social workers must become involved in advocacy and social action, to help resolve systemic or societal problems. . . . There is ample evidence of a high correlation between entry into out-of-home care and social problems such as poverty, deprivation and racism." The Agency did not engage in advocacy at all, whether to improve housing conditions, raise wages, or even reduce anti-Semitism. It was by no means an organization akin to today's Children's Defense Fund, say—advocating social policy but not itself directly helping individual children.

On the contrary, the Agency saw itself as a retail helper, so to speak, intervening with individual families, not to change the social system but to help children find a place in it. Its leaders were willing not just to support foster homes but to make a personal commitment; to sacrifice leisure (although monthly meetings did take the form of luncheons at the Locust Club, the Warwick Hotel, Snellenberger's Restaurant, or even the Rydell Country Club); to visit children themselves and assess foster families; to form personal bonds with those being helped. Their meticulous early records note the name of the child and the name of the visitor: Miss Baum visiting Rose Hymowitz on North 6th; Mrs. Loeb visiting Benjamin Chernicoff on North 15th; Mrs. Zucker visiting Meyer Bachin on

North 31st. They were a small group taking on a big task: there had been 15,000 Jews in Philadelphia in 1880; by 1920, there were 200,000.

The Agency's main strategy was child "placement"—foster care—which it championed as a preferred alternative to life in orphanages. Children in bad circumstances would be taken in by loving families, fairly paid for their effort. As a 1919 Russell Sage Foundation report put it: "Child-placing in families was the most important development in child welfare work during the latter half of the 19th century." But controversy over it still raged during the Agency's early years. Advocates of institutional care remained powerful and were quick to note that institutional care allowed for large-scale recreation and education programs, for cleanliness and efficiency, and for ease of inspection by those paying the bills. By contrast, wrote Superintendent R. R. Reeder of the New York Orphan Asylum at Hastings-on-Hudson in 1918, "The most secluded institution in the world is the private home. It is ten times more difficult to find out what takes place behind its closed doors than it is to probe the methods and secrets of institutions."

The Juvenile Aid Society's solution to the inevitable danger of child abuse in private homes—a problem that plagues those involved in child protection in our own era of widespread foster care—rested on the personal efforts of the Agency's own home-finding and placement committees. These volunteers, complemented by a small paid staff, personally reviewed each family history, inspected potential foster homes, and paid monthly visits to children in their care at the homes in which they'd been placed. Its home-finding committee rejected twice as many potential placement homes as it approved: it required Agency children to have their own rooms. Each board member visited thirty to forty children each month.

Agency reports make clear that its representatives understood what a difficult task they were imposing on foster mothers—at times even recommending higher than the normal $4.50-per-week board payment for the placement of difficult children, presaging the "special needs" consciousness of our own time. The Agency readily increased its payment to the foster mother of the "mischievous" Bass boys, ages eight and thirteen, from $22 to $25 a month, for instance, and it granted an increase as well to Jack Ginsburg's foster mother, in view of his mental retardation and bed-wetting.

Twenty-three years after the Agency's birth, founding director Matilda Kohn Sternberger first visited Bernard Husock and his elder sister, of 2328 South 3rd Street. The heiress to a fortune her mother's family had made selling Civil War uniforms to both sides, Mrs. Sternberger was by then widowed and had given up the grand mansion on 15th Street, where she'd lived with her husband, to share an apartment with her sister Dorothy, also widowed, at 250 South 17th Street, just off Rittenhouse Square. Then, as now, it was among Philadelphia's best addresses, boasting a doorman and, out front, four cast-iron hitching posts. Throughout their more than forty years of widowhood, both sisters wore black, a grandnephew recalls; often it was black bombazine, which crackled when they moved. Both were "forces of nature," the grandnephew says; they were "a stiff set—strong-willed, formal, and Victorian." They were "T.R. Republicans, not liberals; F.D.R., to them, was the antichrist." Both were avid trout fishermen; Mrs. Sternberger directed that her ashes be scattered over her favorite fishing spot on Lake Placid, near her summer home.

There were days, one can imagine, when Mrs. Sternberger came out of 250 South 17th Street to go to lunch at the Sun Dial Tearoom next door—other days when she would call for her driver to take her to South Philadelphia. To judge by Agency records, this woman of means was devoting far more time to home visits to foster children than to lunch at the Tearoom, however. She routinely supervised thirty children and sometimes reported more visits than that in a given month. By the time she met my father and his sister, she had been engaged in such visits herself for more than twenty years and, not unjustifiably, had by 1935 come to list her occupation in city records as "social worker." Her special interest, Agency records show, was adolescent girls.

The chain of events that brought their lives together, a young brother and sister and Mrs. Sternberger, began with a private drama in the Ukrainian village of Brzne, where in 1910 my father's mother, Leebe Przkylnik, gave birth to a baby girl. Still alive today at eighty-nine, my father's elder half-sister all but acknowledges her own illegitimacy. Although she refers to her mother as "divorced," she says, plainly, "My mother was impregnated by the son of a wealthy family, who then left her." Need can arise from acts of God or personal mistakes—both causes seem to have led to my father's predicament. His mother left the Ukraine in 1912, leaving her young daughter with her own mother. She was put in touch with a man from Brzne, then living in Philadelphia—forty-year-old Abraham Chusid (sometimes Husick or Chased, and ultimately, Husock), a widower with two older children. By 1920, these two slightly shopworn characters were married.

He was a presser in clothing plants on Philadelphia's Arch Street, which housed dozens of small, family-owned firms in four- and five-story buildings—Jaffe Brothers, Canter Brothers, Sol Glaser and Co.—and which today houses similar firms employing Chinese immigrants. Though he spoke only Yiddish, and could not read or write even that, my grandfather was part of Philadelphia's $1-billion-a-year textile industry, largest then of any city in the world. His small share of that wealth could support a lower-middle-class life in the part of North Philadelphia called Strawberry Mansion. There in 1921, with one child, a daughter, already born to them, Reba and Abraham Chased (as they were listed) purchased their own unadorned, plain-front, tan brick row house—2639 North Myrtlewood Street—financed with a $1,400 mortgage from the United Producers Building and Loan. And there, in 1925, my father was born, literally in the house.

It was a tiny street, little wider than an alley, with forty attached houses on the two sides. Its modest residents—small grocers, produce dealers, a tinsmith—were far from Philadelphia's poorest. When my father was born, just over half had their own phones, though not my father's parents. But the household had its elements of gentility and ambition. My grandmother encouraged her eldest child—my father's half-sister, who was finally brought to America—to attend the city's normal school for teachers, rather than its trade school for secretaries. There was a piano and piano lessons for my father's full sister (five years older)—I'll call her Sylvia, since she doesn't want to be named "like those TV talk shows"— who remembers running down Myrtlewood Street to tell her mother about her good report card in the fourth grade, around 1929. Her mother was, at the same time, teaching her to read and write Yiddish.

By 1930, Abe and (now) Lena Husick, as the city address directory listed them, did have their own phone. Abe would later boast of having earned $125 a month. And as important as anything were the small dignities and proper appearances of a striving, middle-class life. Among my father's only memories of his mother—and it is filled with wistfulness—is that of her serving him poached eggs for breakfast, arranged with triangles of toast around the yolks. Little things must have mattered a lot to Lena Husick, to take such care in presenting breakfast to a five-year-old boy.

49

The descent, when it came, was rapid. There had been domestic fights, dishes broken in anger, accusations that my grandfather was not bringing home the money he was earning, and, especially after 1929, spells of unemployment. To my father's sister, their mother was "the pusher, a higher class than he—and that's what caused the terrible turmoil." My grandmother paid an unending price for that terrible mistake in Brzne, that ill-fated affair that had left her with a ne'er-do-well as a husband.

Suddenly, with the Depression under way, there were no prospects: only children and a husband who did not make a living. "Where will I get bread?" she asked, Sylvia now recalls. Abe's earnings had fallen from $125 a month to $10 or $14 a week—when he was able to find work—the Juvenile Aid Society's records would ultimately show. At the same time, my grandmother accused him of having a wandering eye, even of wanting her dead. "When I'm gone you'll be a *frei vogel*," a free bird.

Her decline began with a car crash outside Trenton, on a trip to see relatives in Boston, a crash from which she was carried away, bloodied, on a stretcher—my father's other significant memory of her. Soon thereafter came a breakdown, and she was taken to a place called Byeberry—officially, the Philadelphia Hospital for Mental Diseases—a "spotlessly clean, white and airy" place, housing eighteen hundred men and two thousand women, according to a Juvenile Aid Society report. One must honor this massive public effort to help the mentally ill, rather than leaving them to roam the streets, in the name of compassion. And it is by no means impossible that Lena might have returned to North Myrtlewood Street, though the odds were long. Manic-depressive disorder was well recognized in 1930, though treatment was limited. For some patients, episodes would pass and not recur—and, if protected from themselves during those periods, they could return to their lives.

But my father's mother did not return. Here's how the records of the Juvenile Aid Society put it: "Since the death of their mother, 9/20/30, after two months in the Philadelphia Hospital for Mental Diseases, where the diagnosis was Manic Depressive Psychosis, death being caused by a cardiac and kidney complication, [Bernard and Sylvia] have been shifted from one home to another."

By 1932, the names of Lena and Abe Husick had vanished from the phone book. The United Producers Building and Loan had taken the house on Myrtlewood Street, and city records listed the former owner as "unknown." Once his wife was gone, Sylvia recalls, my grandfather was "helpless"—unable even to prepare his children's meals. He would pace the house, muttering: "*Die kinder* [the children]—who will take care of *die kinder*?" Was it an acknowledgment of the burden of responsibility or simply of his own inability to care for his progeny? Or was it the statement of a straightforward problem: who could he get to take care of them? Ultimately, his state of mind and work habits would matter; the Juvenile Aid Society would not hesitate to come to its own conclusion about them.

When he first "requested a plan" in June 1932—twenty months after his wife's death—the Agency was sympathetic. It regularly provided widowers with support, even with a housekeeper, to hold the household together, and it readily approved his request. But he did not use the money to keep his household together. For a period on Myrtlewood Street, after his wife's death, he had tried that route: he'd hired a Hungarian cook to prepare the meals. But he did not have the money then to keep the cook for long, and another woman, lured into the house by romantic promises, did not stay long, either. By the time he began to receive money from the Agency, perhaps even before he applied for aid, he had left Myrtlewood Street behind.

He had re-married sometime before the end of 1932—whether officially or not, I can't determine—and he had moved his children to the home of his new wife, the former Mrs. Bernstein, in South Philadelphia, a step down in the world from the Strawberry Mansion neighborhood. Presumably, the money from the Agency, once it approved his request for a plan, helped to pay expenses there. His daughter, Sylvia, for her part, has never forgiven him for asking for help. "He was always someone who was looking for something for nothing," she acidly remarks. What he did not know was that he was opening himself to a scrutiny he would never otherwise have faced.

Those members of the Agency's placement committee who reviewed my father's case included Emma Loeb, wife of the developer Arthur Loeb, whose firm had constructed Philadelphia's Broad Street subway line; golf-playing and blue-serge-suited Rosa deYoung, one of Pennsylvania's first elected woman state legislators; and agency co-founder Bella Selig, who was married to the head of a firm called Moss Rose Manufacturing—and who would eventually leave most of her considerable fortune to the Agency. They met twice a month to sort through the families asking for help. We think of immigrant Jews as having been a middle-class-in-waiting; but the records of the Juvenile Aid Society tell stories of greatly troubled families, a group of poor Russians whom these German Jewish ladies with Victorian values were determined to set right, even if it took harsh measures.

There was illegitimacy, as in the case of the five Rosenthal children, whose mother had "led an immoral life," according to the placement committee, having never married the children's father. Unable to keep the kids together, the committee placed two with their grandfather, and provided him with a housekeeper. But when he didn't give them "the supervision and interest they need," the Agency moved them to foster care with strangers.

There was crime. A Mr. Lerner, in Holmesburg Prison, "has never done any legitimate work and was forced to move . . . from New York because he had served three prison terms there and a fourth offense would mean life imprisonment." The "extremely unhappy, neurotic" Mrs. Lerner "has given the children very inadequate care. . . . [They] have never received the love which was their due. Mrs. Lerner hoards her money, even depriving her children of necessities. Miss Baum asked whether Susan could be placed in a finer type of home without fear of over-placement and the worker thought this could be done."

There was desertion. "Mrs. Cautin had deserted the family because of the acute financial situation and the crowded quarters. We learned, however, that this was not her first desertion. . . . Mr. Cautin is genuinely interested in his children and expressed the desire to have them remain with him. It was suggested that, if Mrs. Cautin could be found, the home could be reestablished with the help of the agency."

It was a similar story that the Agency's board considered on March 22, 1934, when it revisited the case of Abe Husock and his children, two years after first approving his plan. The record of that meeting tells the story of a period in my father's life so bleak that he still finds it hard to discuss. He speaks of himself in the third person: "That was a scared little boy." The Agency's records make clear why. "Mr. Husock's third wife had turned them out of the home, because he was unemployed and she was unwilling and unable to care for his children. Both children were very unhappy in the home of their step-mother, who mistreated them." All three, the fifty-five-year-old father with his thirteen-year-old daughter and eight-year-old son, wandered around, with the children boarded, presumably with money from the Agency, in a series of different homes: the Segals, the Spivacks, the Gurewitzes on Cantrell Street—a house with a porch and kids nearby to play with, and a funeral, right there in the house, when Mrs. Gurewitz's father dropped dead helping to carry a refrigerator. Mrs. Gurewitz even came to school to meet my father's teacher when he was having problems in the first grade, in a new school in the new neighborhood.

At other times, Abe Husock apparently did not place his children anywhere. Did he try to make the Agency money support all three of them? Did he have hopes of reconstituting their own household—though he had done little toward that end, having frittered away the $1,100 insurance settlement he ultimately received from his late wife's automobile accident? In those times, all three of them shared a single room. "It was Depression time; he couldn't get a job anywhere," my father recalls. "I remember the crowds of people, 'Who wants to work for 25 cents an hour? Who wants to work for 20 cents an hour?'" Despite it all, my father remembers his father warmly from those times as a man who told him stories and took him to synagogue, and for whom he recalls rolling cigarettes, father and son using the rolling machine together. One of those cigarettes smoldered one evening in Abe Husock's mattress in the boardinghouse where he and his children were staying. When the mattress caught fire, only Sylvia awoke, leading her father and brother, as in a dream, to the street and saving their lives.

There were worse times, when the children did not know where to go home at night at all, including the night when Sylvia led my father across the Walt Whitman Bridge to Camden, New Jersey, where their elder half-sister—by then, a married schoolteacher—would at least provide a meal and a place to sleep. (Had there been no available charity, one wonders, would the half-sister have taken in the two children?) It was a time my father remembers thinking when he awoke in the mornings that it all might turn out to be a child's bad dream, from which he would wake up back on Myrtlewood Street, with his mother serving him poached eggs with triangles of toast.

Instead, his situation came to the attention of the Agency's Placement Committee, meeting in Room 209 of the Jewish Federation Building on 9th Street, in March 1934. The report of the proceedings of that day is a harsh indictment of my grandfather, written by a group willing to judge people unsentimentally—and, backed by laws dating from 1825, to take their children away. Not for them today's doctrine of "family preservation"—trying to keep biological parents and children together at almost all costs. The Agency had already tried that; its board members were fed up with the ways in which my grandfather had been wasting their money.

"Placement is now being requested," reads the report, "because Mr. Husock has proven to be a shiftless, irresponsible person and it is necessary that a permanent plan be made for the children" to give them "a measure of security." Had Abe Husock not frittered away the insurance settlement from his wife's car accident? He had "claim[ed] that this money had been used up in paying the funeral expenses and supporting the children," the report notes—and the operative word here is "claim." It recurs. "Although Mr. Husock claimed to be unemployed, his wife informed us that he works irregularly. . . ." He was supposed to have contributed toward the children's support, the report continues, "but he has not adhered to this plan. It is felt that even if he were working steadily, he would not pay toward the children's support, unless a court order is placed upon him." The best thing for the children, the Agency decided, was to take them away and put them in a foster home.

The Placement Committee believed that it could differentiate among the wide range of supplicants it saw—and, because it was spending private funds, it had the discretion to make such choices, to put the needs of the children first, without unduly worrying about the feelings of the parents or about what today's social workers would call the goal of "implementing more culturally sensitive child-protective services." The Agency did not kid itself that Abe Husock was leading some different, but still valid, way of life.

It viewed him instead as having failed his children—about whom committee members were knowledgeable, indeed enthusiastic. The Agency's assessment sang with praise of my father's sister: Sylvia "is an attractive, extremely intelligent girl," who "does brilliant work," the report gushes. "She has always carried a great deal of the responsibility for Bernard, who is shy and dependent on her." When all else had failed, it was she who had "arranged for Bernard and herself to live in the home of a school mate, where they have made a fine adjustment." This was the Bleischman family, which would take them in and be paid for its trouble by the Agency. Abe Husock's custody of his own children was at an end.

Even after their placement, Sylvia and Bernard continued to visit their father. On New Year's Eve, 1935, the day he died, Sylvia found him, unconscious, on the floor of the rooming house in which he was living above a butcher's shop at 4th and Wolf, in South Philly. He had complained for a while, my father recalls, of rectal pain. When the fifteen-year-old girl and her ten-year-old brother worked their way through the bureaucracy and corridors of the Philadelphia General Hospital the next morning, someone would explain to them in Yiddish that he was *tot*—dead. But the brilliant girl would overhear the doctors and remember sixty-plus years later: prostate hypertrophy, leading to the inability to urinate, with blood poisoning the result—just as it was indicated on the death certificate. One can only wonder whether, had she and her brother been living with him still, they might have saved him—the condition was surgically treatable, even then—and whether there would have been no burial on New Year's Day, 1936, in a pauper's grave, with costs paid for by the burial society to which he belonged. Such was the fate of the shiftless and irresponsible in 1935.

As for me, my middle name is Abel, in memory of Abe; whatever his failings, my father did not fail to honor him, as Jewish custom would have it. And Abe's death provided a warning for me more than sixty years later. Because a physician dutifully listed prostate hypertrophy as the cause of his death, I was led to consider whether that swelling could have been owed to cancer—and to seek the tests that identified my own prostate cancer at the earliest, most treatable stage.

By the time of Abe's death, the agency had arranged a long-term placement for Bernard and Sylvia at the home of a barber and his wife, Louis and Miriam Grisbord, who owned a corner row house at 3rd and Fitzgerald Streets, near the southern edge of South Philly. One factor that made the Agency's placement system work was the fact that low-income Philadelphians commonly weren't apartment dwellers but instead lived in—and owned—row houses. They had mortgages to pay off and, with the Depression, were willing to rent rooms to a variety of comers, foster children included. At the Grisbords, my father fondly remembers a fellow boarder named Martin, an out-of-power Democratic committeeman in a Republican-machine city, who would always dress well and always first demur, when asked if he had plans for dinner, before joining the others.

In keeping with Agency rules, my father and his sister had to have their own rooms, a luxury at the Grisbords, where a married couple with a child boarded together in a single room. My father took advantage of his tiny room to have a desk at which to study and even set up a chemistry set. In other respects, he and his sister were better off than their street-corner peers who were not in the Agency's care. The Agency provided medical care and psychological testing: my father can recall being much affected by hearing the psychologist who tested him, at age ten, remark: "This is a pretty smart kid." There was an arrangement for the children to make annual visits to Hanover Shoes. The Agency sent its wards eggs and milk, beds and bedding, and it paid for two weeks at the Jewish Federation's summer camp. My father's memories include the names of the cabins—each named for a different college, including D for the Drexel Institute of Technology, to which he would eventually take the streetcar from the Grisbords' to attend.

One of the most profound consequences of Sylvia and Bernard's formal placement was the new, far deeper personal relationship that Sylvia developed with Mrs. Sternberger. "I called her my fairy godmother," Sylvia recalls—and sure enough, not only did she visit Sylvia in South Philly, but she spirited her, Eliza Doolittle–style, to 250 South 17th, as well, where German maids waiting at table introduced her to foods and decorum she'd never known. Mrs. Sternberger threw open a closet filled with old clothes that had belonged to her nieces and told Sylvia to pick out what she liked. There were trips to the symphony and to Congregation Rodeph Shalom to be introduced to Jewish society.

Mrs. Sternberger's hope was to lead the children she supervised up the social ladder. For that reason, she didn't like placing children in foster homes where they would get room and board in exchange for domestic work. "I tried [that]," the minutes of a January 1933 board meeting quote her as saying, "but never was successful." And if Mrs. Sternberger made Sylvia a protégée, Sylvia in turn transmitted the values of upward mobility she was learning to her younger brother, urging him to do his homework so that he would not "end up like Poppy." As my father recalls: "That was her big thing with me, 'You'll end up like Poppy; you'll end up like Poppy.'" My father's strongest memory of Mrs. Sternberger's talks with him in the Grisbords' front parlor was her urging that, when he succeeded as an adult, he must always remember his own charitable obligations. "She would recite all these other cases that she had had—other people who had been like me, who had now made it and were big contributors." Her own charities weren't limited to South Philly's kids: at the same time she was meeting with my father, she was making special donations to the Agency to bring Jewish children out of Nazi Germany to foster homes in Philadelphia.

When my father thinks back about what made the difference in his life, though, he doesn't name the Agency first, or even Mrs. Sternberger. "If there's anyone who rescued me," he says, "it was Mrs. Grisbord," the foster mother with whom the Agency placed him. She scrubbed him thoroughly when he arrived in the household. "I remember saying, 'Gee whiz, my fingernails are white.' I never remember having white fingernails before that." She took him to South Street to bargain for a bar-mitzvah suit. ("Let me make a living," the clothier would say. "You don't deserve to make a living!" she would reply.) And she held together a boardinghouse-style household that contributed mightily to his sense of security, even to his ultimate livelihood. Mr. Grisbord, who operated a barbershop in the room fronting the street, brought my father along in the trade, helping him get his license and finding him good-paying work at other shops when he graduated from the South Philadelphia High School for Boys ("Southern") and the Agency no longer contributed to his support. One of the Grisbords' own children, whom Sylvia sought out in later life and regularly took to lunch, remembered my father's childhood laughter as having helped light up her home.

Very much a working-class family—although Mrs. Grisbord subscribed to the *Literary Digest* and Mr. Grisbord listened to opera on the radio—the Grisbords respected, even deferred to, their academically oriented wards. No doubt the Agency had informed them of Sylvia's "brilliance"—dramatically confirmed when, not yet sixteen, she graduated second in her class from the elite Girls High School and went on scholarship to the University of Pennsylvania—as noted on page one of the *Philadelphia Evening Ledger*, which pointed out that the Juvenile Aid Society had assisted her to this pinnacle.

Beyond the Grisbord household, the neighborhood was a rich resource—safe, friendly, and peopled by watchful adults, who congregated up the block at Lazowick's drugstore and who relayed the daily number in loud voices down the street. "Once I had ringworm," my father recalls, "and the woman next door would come and put iodine on it every day—just a neighbor." He was part of a group that played stickball and kick the can in the street and awarded benign nicknames: he was Jupiter, for his interest in astronomy and in Mozart's 41st Symphony. The larger Philadelphia community abounded in institutions that played key roles in his development. His South Philadelphia High School teachers introduced him to the Mozart he still loves and urged him on in Latin and in his "declamations" of Longfellow and the Gettysburg Address. They prepared him for a career requiring him to be at home with calculus, the sciences, and public speaking—with the Agency regularly reviewing his report cards. And the Franklin Institute, a science museum founded through a bequest from Benjamin Franklin, was an inspiration to a boy who followed, as a career, Franklin's own interest in electricity. So it would be possible to understand my father and his sister as having been saved not only by the Agency but also by what Thomas Sowell would call the accumulated cultural capital of the neighborhood.

Still, the Agency was the key to it all, the institution that made everything else possible. Sylvia recalls seeing prostitutes on the street and considering the thin margin between her fate and theirs. Looking back, a generation later, I can't help feeling a debt of gratitude and believing the world would be better if organizations like the Agency still operated today, despite the vast changes between my father's childhood and the present.

The idea that a private philanthropy, largely staffed by volunteers, should take on the delicate task of "child protection" would seem quaintly antique to today's experts, with their now-instinctive belief that the proper response to need should be public, not private. Such experts view the private good works of the Victorians as outworn evolutionary stages toward a world in which "human services" are, rightly, a state responsibility. In the experts' social democratic view, a world of private philanthropy fails the key test of universalism. Back in the Agency's world, they would say, chance and caprice played too great a role in determining which children got which sort of attention. Only a system that gives no child a greater claim on assistance than any other can be just or legitimate.

Moreover, where would a world of private philanthropy leave the minority kids who are today's most usual candidates for help? And why should upper-middle-class blacks inter-vene in the lives of these children, for whose plight the entire society is, in this view, responsible? For Mrs. Sternberger and her colleagues, who didn't blame America for the condition of immigrant Russians, it seemed logical to take charge of the children of their poorer brethren. "When they heard of some-one in trouble," Mrs. Sternberger's grandnephew recalls, "they would automatically ask, 'What can we do?' They couldn't conceive of government playing such a role." But blacks, not illogically, have taken the opposite view—and his-torically, have lacked the financial resources to take on such an effort, anyway. Their biggest attempt in this direction—the Urban League's effort to shape itself as a mass immigrant aid society to acculturate rural blacks to urban life—ended in fail-ure after World War I. With all these impulses pushing toward publicly funded, universally available social-service pro-grams, it's no wonder that the powerful child-oriented non-profit agencies of today—above all the Children's Defense Fund—are not themselves providers of services but rather ad-vocates for greater public funding of child-welfare services.

Yet in practice, the replacement of private charities with public departments of child welfare has been far from an un-mitigated improvement. The child protection these agencies provide is universal only in theory. Horror stories of child abuse and neglect unchecked by publicly paid social-service providers raise the question of whether the public system can ever offer the benefits that come with the individual, charita-bly motivated interest of a Mrs. Sternberger coming to the par-lor. Any big-city tabloid almost any week prints the by-now familiar litany of children burned, beaten, starved, or killed by parents, foster parents, or mothers' boyfriends in households supposedly under the supervision of public agencies that have repeatedly failed to conduct the required home inspections—or didn't understand what they were seeing when they did. It hasn't been demonstrated that public institutions are capable of providing the effective inspections that the reformers who originally pushed for foster care understood as key to the system.

If the goal of universalism in child protection is a chimera, no matter how much money we pour into our public systems—if no public system can provide the oversight that private, often religiously motivated, groups, operating on their own rather than through government contracts, provided in their day—perhaps it's time to consider whether we could, and should, return to a Juvenile Aid Society approach to assist the children of today's minority urban poor. Perhaps we could resuscitate the powerful philanthropic and volunteer impulses, and the institutions of civil society, that an expanded welfare state has stifled.

How practical would such an approach to child protection really be today? For the first time in American history, blacks have accumulated significant wealth, and Michael Jordan has set the example of endowing a foundation for children in Chicago. Well-established mega-churches could organize volunteers, much as Congregation Rodeph Shalom did for the Juvenile Aid Society. For example, despite a national foster-home shortage, a Chicago program called "One Church, One Child," in which ministers appeal for foster parents from the pulpit, has been dramatically successful in finding homes for formerly hard-to-place black children.

Organizing such efforts by race or ethnicity suggests itself because, historically, ethnic group members have been those most motivated to take care of their brethren. But these efforts could be organized by locale as well, with towns taking care of their own through local foundations. A true inheritor of the Juvenile Aid Society tradition would need only embrace the idea of the affluent giving their time and resources to uplift poor children—to teach them "moral behavior" through "right habits and daily practice," as the Agency put it. It would stress the personal nature of the transaction, as well as the discretion to withhold or condition support. Nor would such non-public efforts have to be small or local: consider the Red Cross, which does not receive government funds but which, with its tacit government franchise to do disaster relief work, has a vast capacity to raise private donations and mobilize volunteers. The fact that we have taken the public route in approaching child protection does not mean that the choice was inevitable—or that the broader welfare state is an historical inevitability that cannot be undone.

From the libertarian side, one could object that any large-scale intervention in the lives of the poor—whether with private or public funds—entails an inevitable danger of dependency. But it does not undermine the market to use charity and volunteers to help prepare people—particularly, children—to take their place in a market-based society. As the Victorians understood—whether in their crusades against drink or promiscuity—civic leaders have a responsibility to help prepare the poor, particularly those not accustomed to urban life, for the trials of the market, rather than simply to let the market discipline their efforts and foreclose opportunity for their children. When the children realize their potential, the whole society benefits.

What this responsibility does not imply, however, is a professional class of publicly funded social-service workers. In fact, the involvement of the successful in assisting the striving guards against the tendency of social-service professionals to blame "the system" for misfortune and to deliver that self-defeating, passivity-inducing message to the poor. In my father's case, that was left to the neighborhood socialists, of whom there was no shortage. He ultimately rejected them; whether with Mrs. Sternberger's advice in mind or not, I cannot say.

For my father, his sister, Mrs. Sternberger, and the Agency, there is a coda to the saga, and not an entirely happy one. Trial and tragedy leave a residue that doesn't evaporate. My father and his sister both went on to successful lives in the upper middle class: my father became an engineer; his sister was a technical and scientific writer who worked for the Environmental Protection Agency and married a candy and tobacco wholesaler who became a successful investor. But brother and sister drifted apart, perhaps because they reminded each other of the trials they had jointly endured, and they have seldom spoken to each other since those hard years. My father went to engineering school on the GI bill— but not until, before entering the navy, he paid his crucial first-semester tuition bill with a private $100 loan from Mrs. Sternberger. He had nowhere else to turn for the money and so went to 250 South 17th to ask for it.

Mrs. Sternberger, for her part, tried to stay in touch with Sylvia—even visiting her at her new home on Philadelphia's Main Line, where, Cinderella-like, she had arrived as a married woman in the late 1940s. But Sylvia, rebuffing her efforts to remain close and to find in her, perhaps, the child the old widow never had, gradually cut off contact, not wanting to be reminded of the past. "I was very cruel to her," Sylvia says today. And my father, notwithstanding his sister's entreaties, never did get around to paying Mrs. Sternberger back the $100, although he had saved enough in the navy to do so. Perhaps he viewed the loan as his due; anyway, he reasoned, Mrs. Sternberger didn't need the money.

Still, as a child I was always struck by the energetic effort he put in each year—uncharacteristic for a man uninvolved in local affairs or institutions—to raise money for the Cleveland Jewish Welfare Fund. Nor did Sylvia entirely forget the advice of her benefactress, either. Even today, in her late seventies, she continues to volunteer, traveling to South Philadelphia to teach English to new Asian immigrants—often passing by the Grisbords' old house on her way. Nor did she fail to attend Mrs. Sternberger's funeral in 1950 at Congregation Rodeph Shalom, where she remembers the reading, presumably at the onetime friendly visitor's own request, of Tennyson's "Crossing the Bar," a perfect poem for a Jewish Victorian who had lived its message of a life guided by religious duty:

> *Twilight and evening bell,*
> *And after that the dark!*
> *And may there be no sadness of farewell,*
> *When I embark;*
> *For though from out our bourne of Time and Place*
> *The flood may bear me far;*
> *I hope to see my Pilot face to face*
> *When I have crossed the bar.*

The Juvenile Aid Society carried on for some years after dealing with my father's case. Chairwoman Bella Selig, one of its founders and main benefactors, passed the torch to Mrs. Lessing Rosenwald, married to the son of Sears magnate and renowned philanthropist Julius Rosenwald. But ironically, largely through the efforts of its limited but always-present paid staff (predominantly Eastern European rather than German Jews), the Agency became an advocate of the forces that ultimately diminished its usefulness. Even when funds were scarce, it contributed monthly to the American Association for Labor Legislation, a key lobbying group promoting passage of the Social Security Act; the Agency's executive director, Gertrude Dubinsky, received personal thanks from I. M. Rubinow, one of the nation's leading advocates for social insurance and the nascent welfare state. The Agency's minutes reflect a faith that as an expanded public sector subsumed efforts such as its own, social services could only improve.

By 1942, the Agency had been merged into a Philadelphia-wide Association for Jewish Children, and ultimately it became part of the Jewish Children's and Family Service, provider of a great range of assistance to many—including 325 children it places, under county contract, in foster care. Some things have changed but little: the rabbi from Congregation Rodeph Shalom sits—as always—on the board of directors, and there are board members whose families have been playing a similar role for four generations, including a nephew of Mrs. Sternberger's. Because the Agency has chosen to obtain only a third of its $9 million annual budget from government contracts, it can continue to emphasize sectarian services for Jews in most of its programs. It even continues to receive funds from the estates of some of the board members of my father's era—including, as recently as 1993, $23,000 from the sale of utility stock that had belonged to the estate of Matilda K. Sternberger. The money, Mrs. Sternberger dictated, should go toward the purchase of radios, televisions, books for the blind, or other recreational devices—for the infirm elderly. One can only speculate whether her lifelong interest in children had waned because of what might have been her own lonely last years, her friendly visiting days over—or whether she was saddened by the unwillingness of her protégés to let her play a role with their own children.

Mrs. Sternberger had anticipated the Agency's future emphasis; today, it assists some 4,000 Jewish elderly each year and employs some 500 volunteers as friendly visitors to them. But it no longer uses volunteers to visit the 325 children (only ten of them Jewish) for whom it cares, and it must not incorporate religion into its approach to those children. Family Service executive vice president Harold Goldman, warm and enthusiastic and well versed in his agency's history, believes that volunteers would have little to offer the black and Hispanic children of drug-addicted mothers for whom the Agency's paid staff now cares. "The cultural barriers are just too great," he says.

Perhaps so. But one wonders whether they are any greater than those that separated two orphaned children in South Philadelphia from a woman arriving in her black Cadillac sixty-five years ago.

[1999]

Leo Trachtenberg

Philanthropy That Worked

OF ALL New York's experiments in helping the poor, few succeeded more resoundingly than the one that sprang from the
alliance of the great Jewish-American financier Jacob Henry
Schiff and a singular young woman named Lillian Wald. They
met in the summer of 1893. In the years that followed, they established a model of private philanthropy and self-help that,
without yielding power to bureaucrats, public or private,
helped sustain the hundreds of thousands of Jewish immigrants who began inundating the Lower East Side around
1880. Their collaboration produced enduring institutions—the
Visiting Nurse Service of New York and the Henry Street Settlement—that still minister to the people of New York. It was
an alliance that in our own time of extensive immigration can

serve as an object lesson in effective philanthropy that uplifts the poor instead of making them dependent.

One summer evening in 1893, Lillian Wald arrived at the imposing East 38th Street town house of Schiff's mother-in-law, Mrs. Betty Loeb—the wife of Solomon Loeb, co-founder of the now legendary Kuhn, Loeb & Co. investment banking house. With her son-in-law, Mrs. Loeb had been supporting a "Sabbath School" on Henry Street—one of the many ways prosperous uptown German-American Jews had found of helping their needy, recently arrived downtown co-religionists. The school taught poor, uneducated, immigrant women basic hygiene, sanitation, and home nursing, badly needed on the Lower East Side. Wald, a volunteer teacher at the school, had come to Mrs. Loeb on the advice of a mutual acquaintance to ask if she and Schiff might be willing to help in a novel endeavor she was planning.

Born in Cincinnati in 1867 to prosperous German-Polish-Jewish immigrant parents, Lillian Wald grew up in Rochester, New York, where her father thrived in the optical goods business. At Miss Cruttenden's English-French Boarding and Day School for Young Ladies and Little Girls, she was a good student: bright, ambitious, and markedly inquisitive. Still, Vassar turned her down when she tried to enroll at sixteen; she was too young, the college explained.

When her older sister Julia was pregnant, Lillian made friends with the Bellevue-trained nurse who looked after her and at once decided that nursing was the career for her, too. "My life hitherto has been—I presume—the type of young American womanhood . . . such as practical mothers consider essential to a daughter's education," she wrote to Irene Sutliffe, the director of nurses at New York Hospital, when applying for training in 1889 at age twenty-two. "This does not satisfy me now. I feel the need for serious, definite work, a need more apparent since the desire to become a professional nurse has made birth."

She graduated from New York Hospital's nursing school in 1891 and for about a year served as a nurse at the Juvenile Asylum on 176th Street—unhappily, for she disapproved of the often callous treatment of the children in the orphanage for homeless immigrants. She quit to enroll in the Women's Medical College, near Stuyvesant Square, but never earned her M.D.: while studying medicine, her life changed when she volunteered to teach at the Sabbath School.

Seated in buoyant and bustling Betty Loeb's opulent parlor that summer evening, Wald laid out the plan she had conceived and asked for money to turn it into a reality. She had experienced, she explained, a kind of epiphany, which she later described in her 1915 book, *The House on Henry Street*, widely used thereafter as a teaching text in nursing, sociology, and social welfare. "A sick woman (Mrs. Lipsky), in a squalid rear apartment . . . determined me, within half an hour, to live on the East Side," Wald wrote. "[A] little girl led me . . . over broken roadways . . . between tall, reeking houses, . . . past odorous fishstands, . . . past evil-smelling, uncovered garbage cans, . . . across a court where open and unscreened closets [toilets] were promiscuously used by men and women . . . and finally into the sickroom." Wald described how she had helped "the sick woman on a wretched, unclean bed soiled with a hemorrhage two days old." The woman was the mother in a family of seven (plus boarders), living in two poverty-stricken rooms. "At the end of my ministrations they kissed my hands," Wald recounted. "That morning's experience was a baptism of fire. . . . I rejoiced that I had had training in the care of the sick that . . . would give me an organic relationship to the neighborhood in which this awakening had come."

71

What she intended, Wald told the intrigued Mrs. Loeb, was to leave medical school to live on the Lower East Side. There, in association with another nurse, Mary Brewster (a direct descendant of Pilgrim leader Elder William Brewster), she would provide nursing care to the poor, regardless of their ability to pay. Would Mrs. Loeb and Mr. Schiff help?

Years later Betty Loeb's daughter, Nina, remembered her mother saying, "I have had a wonderful experience. I have just been talking to a young woman who's either crazy or a great genius." Lillian Wald wasn't crazy. In fact, she was about to create the entirely new field of public health nursing. All through her life she affected potential supporters as powerfully as she affected Betty Loeb that day. As a 1929 *New Yorker* profile put it: She "is exalted in after-dinner oratory; her good works are applauded by bankers, social leaders, Tammany sachems, Republican statesmen, and nice old ladies."

Without hesitation, Betty Loeb promised to help, a promise that affected Lillian Wald's life, the lives of thousands of residents on the East Side, and, in a signal way, the life of Jacob Schiff.

Like the Jews on the Lower East Side, Schiff, too, had come to an alien land when, in 1865, he arrived in America from Frankfurt am Main at eighteen. In 1893 he was forty-five, rich, and influential, with a reputation on Wall Street, in corporate boardrooms, and in government ministries as a master of finance.

Always carefully dressed, his graying beard neatly trimmed, a flower usually gracing his jacket lapel, Schiff was serious, uncommonly intelligent, opinionated, and principled. Only five feet two inches, he was a commanding presence: "Though small in size," it was said of him, "his presence seemed to fill the largest doorway when he appeared. You had only to look once into those blue eyes to know he was someone to be reckoned with."

Schiff had an encyclopedic understanding of the byzantine, rapidly expanding American railroad system. The word on him was, "He carries every railroad in the country, every bit of rolling stock, every foot of track, and every man connected with each line—from the president down to the last brakeman—inside his head."

In 1901 he would stalemate the lordly J. P. Morgan in a titanic Wall Street battle to wrest control of the Northern Pacific Railroad away from Morgan's client, the breezy, slippery James J. Hill. Schiff represented E. T. Harriman, peevish, always sick-looking—and seething with dislike for Hill. When Hill moved to acquire the Chicago, Burlington & Quincy system, Ned Harriman took alarm: control of the CB&Q would put Hill in a position to block Harriman's eastern-based railroad empire from access to Chicago. Harriman and Schiff asked for shares in the CB&Q, a request Hill dismissed. In response, Harriman, with Schiff's backing, decided to snatch control of Hill's more important Northern Pacific. It was a bold and astonishing gambit.

Schiff and Harriman began buying Northern Pacific stock in April and May at around $90; so did Hill and Morgan. The stock shot up; short-selling speculators moved in. Soon the shorts were frantically competing for stock to cover their positions as Northern Pacific's price zoomed to an absurd $1,000 a share. Finally, there was no stock left to buy: a classic corner had ensued. When—inevitably—the bubble burst and Northern's price plummeted, the rest of the market joined the rout, triggering the worst Wall Street panic in a hundred years. In November the warring factions declared an armistice. Hill and Harriman agreed to share seats on the board of a holding company controlling the Northern Pacific and the railroads linked with it, including the CB&Q. Afterward, Morgan, ever the realist, acknowledged Schiff as his only equal (though hitherto he had disdainfully called him "that foreigner").

73

But multiplying his fortune wasn't Jacob Schiff's sole purpose in life. Pious, proud of his descent from a distinguished line that included rabbis and scholars and that reached back to the fourteenth century, Schiff took seriously his obligation to the less fortunate. Throughout his life he gave the Talmudic 10 percent—and, when necessary, more—of his large earnings to charity. The prayer that preceded Friday evening family meals at his home concluded: "Continue to bless us with Thy mercy, so that we may be able to share our own plenty with those less fortunate than ourselves."

Talk is cheap, of course. But from the evidence of his works, Schiff meant what he said: his philanthropies were numerous and unfailing. Though much, probably most, of his charity went to Jewish causes—Montefiore Home for Incurables (which became Montefiore Hospital), the Hebrew Aid Society, Mount Sinai Hospital, among others—by the time he died he had also given large sums to such non-Jewish causes as Barnard College, Harvard University, and the American Red Cross.

The money that Lillian Wald required wasn't much compared with Schiff's major benefactions, and upon hearing Wald's plan, the financier, by then senior partner at Kuhn, Loeb & Co., agreed to share with Mrs. Loeb the expense of supporting the two nurses and to supply them with doctors when needed. But the donation marked the start of a close, twenty-seven-year special relationship between the tycoon and the idealistic, enterprising nurse. It was so close that on the day of the Northern Pacific battle with Morgan, with Wall Street consumed by panic, Schiff phoned the startled Wald to say, "I think this is the night Mrs. Schiff and I were coming down to take dinner. Is the hour six or half past six?"

By supporting Wald, the often imperious Jacob Schiff linked himself to a woman whose compelling personality in important ways complemented his own. Schiff understood the uses of power; in both business and family matters, he could be unyielding or compromising as circumstances required. His ultimate aim was to get the job done, whether it was supporting and supervising philanthropies or financing a railroad. From the beginning of his relationship with Wald, Schiff noted traits that he himself possessed: intelligence, single-minded devotion to work, effectiveness in carrying out a mission. He saw in Wald an ally in his most cherished philanthropic cause: strengthening the Jewish community by helping new immigrants weather their immediate crises and then gain the tools to help themselves.

Beginning in the 1880s, a flood of Jews escaping the grinding poverty and anti-Semitism of eastern Europe and the brutal Russian pogroms poured through Ellis Island into the Lower East Side. They brought with them meager belongings, an abundance of hope, and a willingness to work hard—hoping, as aspiring immigrants do today, to make a life in a country that, for all its imperfections, was a land of freedom and opportunity. Indeed, much of today's thriving Jewish middle and upper-middle class is descended from immigrants who arrived in that fusion of poverty and striving.

Photos of the neighborhood at that time show us pushcart commerce clogging the streets amid shawled women and bearded men. The clamors of peddlers ascended, and the pervasive smells of food hawked from pushcarts mingled with the shouts of raucous children. With its blocks of begrimed tenements, the area resembled a crowded ghetto transplanted from the despotisms of eastern Europe to the City of New York.

Of the 1.5 million people living in Manhattan in 1893, 5 out of 6 lived in tenements, many under unhealthful conditions. An annual death rate of 26 per 1,000 prevailed in the borough, twice what it would be fifty years later. In the worst tenements it was much higher. Tuberculosis, the "white plague," was a constant and pervasive threat among the Jews, because many of them worked in poorly ventilated, unsanitary needle-trade sweatshops, an environment in which the bacillus thrived. Indeed, many called TB the "tailor's disease."

The tenements in which they lived weren't much healthier. "They are great prison-like structures of brick," according to a November 1888 article in *The American Magazine*, "with narrow doors and windows, cramped passages and rickety stairs. They are built through from one street to the other with a somewhat narrow building connecting them. . . . The narrow courtyard . . . in the middle is a damp, foul-smelling place, supposed to do duty as an airshaft: had the foul fiend designed these great barracks they could not have been more villainously arranged to avoid any chance of ventilation. . . . In case of fire they would be death-traps." During July and August, tenants suffered from debilitating heat, intensified by coal-burning stoves, gas jets, and steam boilers. During a nine-day August heat wave in 1896, 420 city residents died from tainted, stifling air.

Not until 1901, when the city established the Tenement House Department, did the law compel better ventilation in new tenements. Lillian Wald and Jacob Schiff were prominent among those pressing the city government for such improvements: decent housing was always one of Wald's primary concerns, and from 1889 onward, Schiff continually denounced slum housing and used his influence to encourage legislation to eliminate or improve deteriorated tenements.

Historian Moses Rischin writes: "By 1890 the Lower East Side bristled with Jews. . . . Exceeding 700 persons per acre, in 1900 the Tenth Ward was the most densely populated spot in the city." During the depression of the 1890s, with jobs scarce, evictions for non-payment of rent were common. "In the year 1891–1892 alone," Rischin recounts, "in two judicial districts of the Lower East Side 11,550 dispossess warrants were issued."

Many of the evicted who had a little money became boarders in the already overcrowded tenement apartments. "At the hour of retiring," as a witness before the U.S. Immigration Commission testified, "cots or folded beds and in many instances mattresses are spread about the floor, resembling . . . a lot of bunks in the steerage of an ocean steamer." When Wald heard of eviction cases she often brought them to the United Hebrew Charities, a favorite Schiff cause, which frequently paid the rents outright or helped with a temporary loan.

The recently arrived immigrants were for the most part law-abiding, but around the turn of the century, some of their Americanized first-generation children fell into the gambling, loan-sharking, burglary, and prostitution rackets. The Lexow and Mazet investigations of the 1890s exposed schemes to turn the East Side into "a Klondike . . . a center of graft and illicit business," according to Rischin.

"Was he Jewish?" was the anxious question Jewish parents often asked when the cops seized a hoodlum. Or they sorrowfully shook their heads when the names of Jewish criminals hit the papers. "In 1909," Rischin writes, "some 3,000 Jewish children were brought before Juvenile Court, and in the next few years Jewish criminals regularly made headlines."

Disturbed by the outbreak of criminal behavior among young Jews, in 1907 Schiff and other German-American Jews founded the Hawthorne School of the Jewish Protectory and Aid Society in upstate New York. The school tried to thwart juvenile delinquency by teaching useful trades—carpentry, printing, plumbing, bricklaying—along with standard class-room courses and the basics of Judaism. Hawthorne succeeded only partially, however; for years the crime problem continued to simmer on the Lower East Side.

Schiff and other prominent Jews took further measures. They established the Kehilla, a self-help group (*kehilla* means "community" in Hebrew) committed to resisting the anti-Semitism that Jewish criminals engendered. It created an intelligence system (which the city administration approved) to ferret out Jewish felons. It also campaigned for a central Jewish philanthropic authority and set up a mediation system for the largely Jewish garment industry. As a social force the Kehilla lasted for about ten years, waning as Jews rose gradually into the middle class and as open-ended Jewish immigration ceased after World War I.

Wald and Brewster's "organic relationship" to the Lower East Side began in September 1893, when they moved into a small fifth-floor walk-up in an old tenement at 27 Jefferson Street and started offering free nursing help to their immigrant neighbors. Soon word got around that two nurses living in the neighborhood would provide help with medical and, inevitably, other problems. Many families lacked clothing; others needed food. Wald and Brewster tried not to fail their sick and indigent neighbors.

They nursed the infirm, arranged for doctors when necessary, and took patients to hospitals. Those needing food or clothing for their families invariably—with Jacob Schiff and United Hebrew Charities providing money—received it. With additional assistance from hospitals, newspapers, and sympathetic individuals, Wald and Brewster gave the afflicted and their families sterilized milk, medicine, food, and—essential in an era without refrigerators—ice. The pioneer nurses became a familiar sight on the Lower East Side, and 27 Jefferson

Street became a place where "workers in philanthropy, clergy-men, Orthodox Rabbis, the unemployed, anxious parents, girls in distress, troublesome boys, came as individuals to see us," Wald wrote. Those visits energized and inspired the two nurses, despite the exhausting demands on them; from the start, Wald and Brewster knew they were a vital and sustaining force in their chosen neighborhood.

Wald became a power on the Lower East Side, recognized by politicians (including influential Tammany pols), cops, neighbors, and street people as committed and incorruptible. "Her slightest wish is accorded a respect which is never accorded the law," reported the *New York Press* in an early story about her. "The would-be violator of sanitary regulations calls her 'Boss Croker' [the Tammany leader], or 'She-Who-Must-Be-Obeyed.'"

To put an official mark on their nursing rounds, Wald asked Schiff to persuade the Board of Health to let her and Brewster wear badges stating they were "Visiting Nurses Under the Auspices of the Board of Health." This was the start of New York's Visiting Nurse Service, which officially incorporated in the 1940s and which now has 23,000 active cases per day. The medallions, and Wald's and Brewster's nurse uniforms, helped open the doors of sufferers inclined to mistrust them.

For Jews were no more immune to the ignorance that often accompanied disease than were other immigrant groups. Some feared that if they were hospitalized, they'd have to drink the contents of a secret (and wholly mythical) black bottle that would put them out of their misery forever. Others suspected that the two nurses might try to convert them to Christianity.

But most immigrants gratefully opened their doors to Wald and Brewster—revealing the harsh texture of life in the slums. Heaps of refuse and swill on floors, children "scarred with vermin bites," adults suffering from typhoid, a pregnant mother living on crusts of bread, TB sufferers—these were typical cases Wald and Brewster came upon.

At the end of a long day of climbing stairs in slum tenements, of coping with filth and disease, of getting food and clothing for hungry families, the two nurses would retreat to their Jefferson Street apartment. There Wald began her routine of writing case reports and sending them to Schiff.

Years later she recalled: "I sat in the kitchen of our little apartment with my feet in the oven, as it was too cold to hold a pen in the frigid temperature of the room, and when the letter was written I went down the many flights of stairs and mailed it in the post box." Over one hundred years after she wrote them, Wald's affecting reports to Schiff give us vivid pictures of conditions in the Lower East Side slums. Unlike the stiffer style of her letters and *The House on Henry Street*, the tone of Wald's reports to Schiff is pithy and free, reflecting a woman happily immersed in a career central to her life, "called" to a great work. Schiff had agreed to support the nurses for at least six months; certainly Wald must have guessed that upon reading her reports he would be moved to continue his support well beyond that period.

"Meyer P., age 5 years, . . . injured his hip. He lay for 7 months in the Orthopedic Hospital . . . was discharged as incurable. . . . [T]he cripple is in pain and cries to be carried. . . . They [Meyer's family] had no rooms of their own but paid $3 a month to Hannah H . . . who allowed the family to sleep on the floor." Upon Schiff's request, the Montefiore Home admitted Meyer. "We have found several cases of typhoid fever, and in every house succeeded in overcoming hospital prejudice, accompanying the patients to the hospital wards to satisfy their first uneasiness."

"Lily Klein very ill with pneumonia for whom we procured medical attention and nursed. The child died, but the night before Miss Brewster had remained with the child all night. . . . Father deserted and mother worn out."

"Visit and care of typhoid patient, 182 Ludlow Street."

"Visit to 7 Hester Street where in rooms of Nathan S. found two children with measles. After much argument succeeded in bathing these two patients and the sick baby. . . . Brought clean dresses to the older children."

"Four people slept in the unlighted room on rags, coats, etc."

"Gave tickets for Hebrew Sanitarium excursion . . . to Mrs. Schneider and 5 children . . . but five of the seven children are nearly naked. . . . So we will make their decent appearance possible."

"7 p.m. visit to Mrs. Lanowitz, took her flowers, clean bedding, made egg-nog and left her in nursing condition for the night."

"Mrs. Jacobson and her two children homeless, without work. We succeeded in placing her for a few weeks at the Children's Aid Society and found a place for the children while she worked."

"In a rear tenement, top floor, . . . a doctor found . . . Mrs. Weichert, crazy and ill with pneumonia and typhoid; [we] cared for her fourteen year old daughter. [Mrs. Weichert] died in a few days, I shall always be glad that the doctor told us in time so she was made human and decent."

"Many of these people have kept from begging and it is not uncommon to meet families, to whom not a dollar has come in seven months—the pawn shops telling the progress of their fall, beginning some months back with the pawning of a gold watch, ending with a woman's waist."

Mary Brewster's health soon broke down. She left the

Lower East Side, married, and died while still young. Little more is known about her. But Wald, more robust, carried on, buoyed by the realization that she had found her true purpose in life.

Wald's work was exactly the kind of philanthropy that Schiff believed worthwhile. It was face-to-face, and it aimed at helping people to help themselves if they possibly could. "Charity and philanthropy to be effective," Schiff wrote in an 1893 memorandum, " . . . should have personal supervision, for it is unlikely that others can carry into practical effect our ideas and intentions as well as we can ourselves."

Just as he knew the details of all those railroads he successfully financed, so he insisted on knowing the truth about the many people or institutions that came to him for help. "If it was an individual," his biographer Cyrus Adler wrote, "he would either try some plan of self-help, or, if the person, by reason of bad health or age, was helpless, place him upon a sort of pension roll, which was kept absolutely private and confidential."

But he carefully supervised that private pension roll. In a letter of May 8, 1889, to a "trusted agent," he wrote: "I send you a list of parties who receive monthly checks from me. . . . I would be obliged if . . . you will have their continued worthiness to receive support reported to me." Schiff's philanthropy continually impresses by the personal, hands-on involvement of the man with the causes he aided, so different from the layers of bureaucracy and thickets of paperwork that characterize today's prominent philanthropic foundations.

The Henry Street Settlement, the institution that Wald founded to further her work in 1894, a year after she arrived on the Lower East Side, perfectly embodied her and Schiff's shared belief that, whenever possible, poor people should help themselves. With the demands for her nursing care sharply increased, and with other nurses volunteering to help her and Brewster, she decided to found the settlement house as an efficient center for her work and a way of extending her mission.

The Lower East Side had many settlement houses. Before moving into her Jefferson Street apartment, Wald had lived for two months in the College Settlement, and the settlement idea had influenced her when she decided on her mission in the slums. London's Toynbee Hall (opened in 1884) and Jane Addams's Hull House (founded in Chicago in 1889) provided the settlement house model, which the eminent historian Gertrude Himmelfarb succinctly characterizes in her description of Toynbee Hall: "It did not dispense relief or charity: it dispensed education, culture, and civic amenities. . . . [Settlement workers] were moralists on behalf of the poor, whom they sought to elevate morally, spiritually, culturally, . . . whom, moreover, they assumed to be capable of and desirous of such elevation."

Settlement founders were strikingly young—Wald was twenty-seven when Henry Street opened, Addams twenty-nine when she founded Hull House—and most settlement workers were youthful idealists who volunteered for a year or two. They established kindergartens, thus setting an example for school systems, and taught English and good citizenship to immigrant adults. Settlements campaigned to open schools during evenings to accommodate classes and children's clubs. They established vocational courses and offered music and art classes. Unsurprisingly, radicals who thought only a complete social revolution could solve the problems of the poor derided the settlements; the fiery Emma Goldman scornfully dismissed them as merely "teaching the poor to eat with a fork." But they did incalculable good.

Wald set out to combine all this with her nursing program. She turned to Schiff, who promptly put his hand and checkbook at her service. "I am now looking for a suitable home either in Henry Street or Madison Street," he wrote to Brewster, "which appears under the advice of Miss Wald . . . where the house should be . . . located." He soon bought the house at 265 Henry Street (destined to become world famous); Wald and Brewster moved in and named it "The Nurses' Settlement," which Wald amended a few years later to "The Henry Street Settlement."

Nursing formed the center of the settlement's mission. At Henry Street, mothers and children attended classes in home nursing, simple first aid, home hygiene, and child care. Above all, the new institution brought public health nursing to the Lower East Side's burgeoning immigrant population, assigning nine full-time nurses to cases in 1898, fifteen in 1904, twenty-seven in 1906. By the time Schiff delivered the celebratory address at the settlement's twentieth anniversary in 1914, the institution deserved to celebrate. That year there were seven branches in New York City, seven fresh-air "vacation homes" in rural areas, milk stations dispensing milk to sick children, clinics, and a staff of ninety nurses visiting 200,000 families every year. Those who could pay a modest sum did so; the destitute received care without charge.

To elevate the neighborhood residents "morally, spiritually, and culturally," Wald soon moved into areas beyond nursing. Henry Street became a community center, offering clubs for children and adults, a library, and a backyard children's playground, the first of its kind in the country. When, with Schiff helping fund the purchases, the settlement added buildings at 299, 301, and 303 Henry Street, it also added classes in printmaking, carpentry, dressmaking, machine shop work, and other trades.

Although the creation of public health nursing was

Wald's major achievement, for the rest of her life she threw herself into an astonishing array of causes. City government reform (in which Schiff was so active that some urged him to run for mayor), playgrounds for children, women's suffrage, the peace movement, lectures, arts classes, trade union and strikers' support, the launching of the Neighborhood Playhouse—this is only a partial list of her (and the settlement's) concerns. The NAACP evolved from meetings at Henry Street, at one of which Schiff made a fervent speech on behalf of the guest of honor, W. E. B. DuBois.

Wald was an archetypal activist, a moderate socialist of the Fabian stamp, who served on committees, organized, lectured, testified, wrote—always with good intentions, often with beneficent results. She helped mediate several rancorous strikes involving East Side residents, disputes in which she enlisted Schiff's influence to resolve. The Henry Street Settlement served as nonpartisan ground on which employers and labor met to settle sometimes bitter differences.

Though Schiff deplored what he termed "the union trusts" (his knowledge of certain ruthless railroad and coal mining unions perhaps influenced him), he supported the right of workers to organize and bargain for better conditions. It was, after all, another type of self-help. Biographer Cyrus Adler tells us: "His association with the Henry Street Settlement work and like efforts brought him into . . . personal contact with workingmen. . . . During one strike [probably the 1910 garment workers strike], conditions among the strikers' families were such that the Henry Street Settlement had to give urgent relief every day to many people. [Schiff] authorized the Settlement to do so on his behalf, and to keep an account of the amount expended. Every night he would send a check for the amount expended. At another time, when pickets were being arrested, he conveyed a piece of property to

85

one of the members of the Settlement, to enable that person to give bail for the arrested strikers." Schiff helped settle the strike; Wald then served on the Joint Board of Sanitary Control overseeing the hygienic conditions in the shops. One wonders what Karl Marx would have made of arch-capitalist Jacob Schiff's basic decencies.

As the years passed, Schiff's support of Wald and the settlement never flagged, though he sometimes disagreed with her. Would Schiff ask his lawyer, Mr. Cravath, to compose a letter to members of the bar, advising bequests to the settlement? He would and did. Should more money be invested in the Social Halls Association, which ran Clinton Hall, a "respectable" center for recreation, weddings, and parties? No, insisted the prudent banker; the settlement had invested "almost a quarter of a million, and after five or six years are not even able to earn sufficient . . . to pay interest on [the] debt." Ventures like the association, though well-intentioned, "have only a very qualified value unless they can be established on a business basis." When Schiff took possession of a golf course near his country place in Rumson, New Jersey, he informed Wald, "We hope to arrange a permanent excursion and playground for children's parties."

Schiff sent checks to the settlement for special needs: an additional night nurse willing to enter the dark slum buildings, an obstetrical nurse, increases in nurses' salaries. "[W]hatever you arrange, in conformity with our family's promises," Schiff wrote her, "will be satisfactory."

Schiff seems to have regarded the settlement as his extended family, as a household he was part of. "I cannot begin the New Year any better than . . . to somewhat increase your emergency fund," he wrote in 1911, enclosing a check. In 1912 Wald decided to set up an endowment fund for the long-range financial health of the settlement; she of course approached

Schiff. "You and Mrs. Loeb were the first friends and believers in me, and you have always made me feel that you are a sharer in every aspiration that I had for the safe-guarding of children and care of our sick, as well as in all other things that you have encouraged in me." Would Schiff take the leadership in setting up the endowment? Of course he would.

Schiff insisted that Wald not reveal the extent of his crucial help, a request that might have been influenced by the Talmudic injunction that whoever gives secretly to the poor is blessed sixfold. Wald respected his wishes. In *The House on Henry Street*, Schiff's name doesn't appear, though until he died he was Wald's steadfast contributor, confidant, and advisor.

The extensive Schiff-Wald correspondence reflects the special fondness the world-famous banker and the innovative nurse and social worker had for each other. Schiff wrote to her often—from his office, from a ship on the way to Europe, while traveling in foreign countries, from his various vacation homes. "It was much of a delight to see your dear face once more," he wrote in 1909. "Mrs. Schiff and I are looking forward with much pleasure to dining with you and the family [at Henry Street]," he wrote in another 1909 message. "It was much of a pleasure to get a glance of you at luncheon yesterday, but please husband your strength . . . by not attempting to do too much," cautioned a 1912 letter.

Wald reciprocated Schiff's high regard. "My love to the dear lady [Mrs. Schiff] and to you," Wald signed a 1917 letter. In a long letter the same year, detailing critical public-health-nursing financial needs, Wald closed with, "I send a great deal of love to you and the dear lady." In another 1917 letter she requested, "Please let me know when you and the dear lady want me to come to the country? I am homesick for you both." And, again in that year, she thanked Schiff for a $3,500 check and ended "With loving appreciation of all that you are to me and us."

As Schiff moved into his seventies he became noticeably more weary. By 1920 he was suffering from a heart condition, then less responsive to treatment than today. On September 25, 1920, with his family at his bedside, he died in his home at 905 Fifth Avenue. His passing was front-page news in the *New York Times* and other newspapers. Schiff was mourned by his kin, by his extended Henry Street family, and by people who had never seen or met him but who venerated him for what he had done for those less fortunate.

On the death of her great friend and supporter, Wald, recalling the consequential day in 1893 when she first met Schiff, wrote of her good fortune to be able "to pour into his understanding ears the despair that an inexperienced girl felt [at seeing] the social conditions of people living in the crowded East Side of Manhattan. Immediately did this busy banker respond to the troubled visitor, and thereby started a fellowship in friendship and social interest that for all the years that followed never failed on his part."

Lillian Wald outlived her faithful patron and advisor by twenty years, throwing herself into an endless whirl of committees, meetings, speeches, and world travel to countries that praised and honored her. By the mid-1930s, ill and unable to continue her work, she retired to her country home in what was then rural Westport, Connecticut, and died there on September 1, 1940. She left behind an enduring monument, proof that with the right kind of help people can lift themselves out of poverty and ignorance through education and through their own striving.

[1998]

HEATHER MAC DONALD

Why the Boy Scouts Work

FEELING DISPIRITED about today's youth? Try attending a Boy Scout meeting. You will find a parallel universe to today's vulgar, sexualized youth culture, filled with gestures of some-times unbelievable delicacy and a code of conduct as anachro-nistic as sixteenth-century courtiership.

Take Harlem's Troop 759. Six boys, from tall to small, sit expectantly around a card table in the basement of a red brick church on Morningside Avenue. The gangly senior patrol leader, Osmond Ollennu, a tenth-grade son of Ghanaians, calls the troop to opening ceremonies ("C'mon, men, form a *straight* line!"), and Osmond's little brother leads it in the Pledge of Allegiance, followed by four full-throated repeti-tions of the scout motto ("Be Prepared!") and one scout slogan

89

("Do a Good Turn Daily"). Then Osmond, who is the troop's second-in-command, announces inspection. While the boys stand quietly in line, he gently reties a neckerchief here, straightens a collar there, occasionally whispering a reminder in a boy's ear. The troop's leader, a dignified eighteen-year-old named Henry Lawson, inspects Ollennu in turn.

To anyone familiar with the chaos in New York's inner-city classrooms, such rituals are a little piece of heaven. Though scouting arose in response to a perceived moral crisis in youth nearly a hundred years ago, its founders could not possibly have foreseen how much more desperately their gift to poor, drifting boys would be needed today. In a world lacking structure, where even family may be constantly in flux, scouting provides order—from the weekly meetings with their flag ceremony and scout oath to the little rules of self-presentation, like neckerchief-tying and tucked-in shirts. To boys desperate for authority and discipline, it offers self-control and a clear path toward achievement. Most important, it speaks a language of selflessness and honor to a culture tongue-tied about virtue. It is a ready-made salvation for urban children, complete with that holy grail: self-esteem. Even so, today's cultural elite, offended by scouting's nineteenth-century ethic of manly virtue, has put it right in the line of fire of today's culture wars.

As the nineteenth century ended, men on both sides of the Atlantic worried about boys, especially poor immigrant boys in the teeming cities, who seemed destined for delinquency or poverty. Ernest Thompson Seton, a Canadian naturalist, wildlife painter, and children's author, summed up these anxieties: "It is the exception when we see a boy respectful of his superiors and obedient to his parents . . . handy with tools and capable of taking care of himself, under all circumstances . . . whose life is absolutely governed by the safe old moral standards." Seton looked around for "robust, manly, self-reliant boyhood," and found instead "a lot of flat-chested cigarette smokers, with shaky nerves and a doubtful vitality"—just as his British contemporaries found an alarming number of young men unfit for the draft.

These concerned men responded by creating a host of character-building organizations, the most powerful of which was the Boy Scouts. The organization grew out of Seton's newly created boys' group, the Woodcraft Indians, and the insights of an ebullient British war hero, Robert Baden-Powell. Lord Baden-Powell had returned to England from the Boer War in 1903 to find children devouring a soldiers' scouting manual he had written. Teachers urged him to revise the manual for boys, and Baden-Powell, inspired by Seton's Woodcraft Indians handbook, seized the challenge.

He envisioned a new organization that would draw on wartime scouting lore and ancient codes of chivalry to teach boys the Victorian virtues. King Arthur's Round Table, Baden-Powell understood, resonated in boys' souls, for it symbolized the marriage of strength and goodness, by contrast with today's "gangsta" culture, which defines manliness as violently predatory. The aim of this new organization, Baden-Powell wrote in 1906, "is to develop among boys a power of sympathizing with others, and a spirit of self-sacrifice and patriotism."

Baden-Powell believed that scouting's core virtues of selflessness and the cheerful performance of duty were as valid for the poor as for the upper and middle classes. "Everything on two legs that calls itself a boy has God in him," he insisted, "although he may—through the artificial environment of modern civilization—be the most arrant little thief, liar, and filth-monger unhung. Our job is to give him a chance." Respect for others, without class distinctions, was a scout's universal duty.

Baden-Powell's *Scouting for Boys*, published in 1908, was

an instant hit. It combined the author's whimsical "campfire yarns" and drawings with nature lore and tales of honor. Scouts would progress through a series of ranks by mastering outdoor skills and showing self-reliance and civic-mindedness. Many of the requirements reinforced bourgeois values: to learn thrift, for example, scouts had to earn and bank up to one shilling. Other requirements were exercises in self-cultivation: boys had to memorize the contents of a shop window after a brief period of observation, for example, in order to develop mental discipline and attention to the world outside the all-absorbing adolescent self.

The core of scouting was the scout law and oath. The scout handbook, historian Paul Fussell has observed, is a "book about goodness," and the law is its purest distillate. Its overarching theme is thoughtfulness toward others. A scout is "friendly, courteous, kind, cheerful, brave," in the American phrasing. Explains Baden-Powell: "When in difficulty to know which of two things to do, [the scout] must ask himself, 'Which is my duty?' that is, 'Which is best for other people?'— and do that one." A scout observes traditional rules of chivalry: he is "polite to all, especially to women, children, old people, and the weak and helpless." He must obey an ironclad law of personal integrity: "If a scout were to break his honour by telling a lie . . . he would cease to be a scout—he loses his life," warns Baden-Powell.

Far from being a stern decalogue, Baden-Powell's law contains only positive injunctions. " 'Don't,' of course, is the distinguishing feature and motto of the old-fashioned system of repression; and is a red rag to a boy," he wrote, with his unerring grasp of boy psychology. "It is a challenge to him to do wrong." Far from being the jingoistic martinet that caricaturists make him out to be, Baden-Powell shares many of the views of today's so-called "progressive" educators. He believed that effort, not just achievement, should be rewarded; he made boys each others' teachers and avoided creating a competitive structure in scouting.

Reviewing the American scouting handbook in 1912, a mother reported that "something in me got to its feet and saluted as a cadet salutes a superior officer." It is impossible to avoid the same reaction to the scout law and oath today. "I had hoped my boy would be all these things, and had so admonished him," the reviewer explained. "But these are Scout Laws, mind you, not advice and admonition, not hopes backed by maternal pleadings and fears, but laws, self-imposed when the Scout takes his oath." Unlike today's progressives, Baden-Powell and his contemporaries recognized children's powerful desire for a moral absolute. And he fed boys' hunger for heroism and valor, traits excluded from today's feminist-inspired pantheon of sensitivity and non-judgmentalism.

The scouts spread electrically. "There suddenly appeared in my world," H. G. Wells wrote, just three years after publication of *Scouting for Boys*, "a new sort of little boy—a most agreeable development of the slouching, cunning, cigarette-smoking, town-bred youngster—a small boy in a khaki hat, with bare knees and athletic bearing, earnestly engaged in wholesome and invigorating games—the Boy Scout."

Quickly spanning the globe, scouting almost instantly leaped to America. The first *American Scout Handbook for Boys of 1911*, edited by Ernest Thompson Seton, contains delightful contributions from American naturalists, a section on chivalry that places the Pilgrim Fathers and Abraham Lincoln in the tradition of Sir Lancelot and Sir Galahad, and meaty material on American history and governance. But combined with the Nature empathy—"the love of the green outdoors—the trees, the tree-top singers, the wood-herbs," as Seton's ecstatic prose

93

put it—was the core Victorian ethic of manly altruism, which harmonized perfectly with reigning American values. Chief Scout Citizen Theodore Roosevelt reminded the scouts in 1913 that "manliness in its most rigorous form can be and ought to be accompanied by unselfish consideration for the rights and interests of others."

The American scout oath and law gave a Yankee twist to Baden-Powell's original, excising all his charming British whimsy. The American scout pledges to keep himself "physically strong, mentally awake, and morally straight," and he must obey the injunction to be "brave, clean and reverent." Long before diversity trainers appeared to browbeat America, the scout law urbanely commanded boys to "respect the convictions of others in matters of custom and religion."

Though World War I sealed scouting's status as the premier American youth movement, thanks to the scouts' indefatigable war-bond sales and collection of matériel, American scouting didn't enter its real heyday until after World War II. The scouts thrived "when America believed in itself," painter and Boy Scout illustrator Norman Rockwell recalled. Every two years, the scouts performed a well-publicized national Good Turn, collecting clothes for overseas, practicing conservation, or getting out the vote. Peer pressure pushed toward, not away from, membership.

The 1960s counterculture and the Boy Scouts of America were a train wreck waiting to happen. Here was a supremely patriotic, service- and family-oriented institution suddenly up against a movement celebrating rebellion and declaring "AmeriKKKa" a fascist regime. The official scout response to the assault on everything the scouts stood for was understandably confused. Though a 1968 annual report scoffed at the "impractical flower world of the Hippie," officials worried deeply about that bogus sixties concept, "relevance." They commissioned a survey that asked, "Is Scouting in Tune with the Times?"—and, not surprisingly, learned that the answer was no.

In 1969, membership dropped for the first time in history; it nose-dived throughout the 1970s. The organization responded first with small changes, then big ones, as recounted by scout historian Robert Peterson. The Cub Scouts dropped "To be square" from their Promise. "Boy" was eased out of the official name, which became for a time simply Scouting/USA. And in 1972, the *Scout Handbook* endured a sweeping overhaul. Gone were such stalwart features as tracking skills, canoeing, rope lashing, and first aid for sunstroke and frostbite. In their place were first aid for rat bites, hiking in the city, and advice on drug abuse. A boy could now reach Eagle rank without ever venturing beyond city limits. No longer a sage on outdoor craft, the scoutmaster became a "personal growth" counselor.

The change in part grew out of the scouts' new emphasis on minority recruitment. In the first half of the century, the Boy Scouts conformed to America's racial caste system, encouraging local councils to form black troops but not insisting that troops be integrated. Black scouts' camping facilities were painfully substandard. Nevertheless, many blacks fondly remember their scouting experiences from the 1940s and 1950s. "It was a thing of pride to wear your uniform on the streets," recalls Harvey Johnson, a scout at the Harlem Boys Club at 134th Street during the late 1940s. "Now, if you try to do it, it's unbelievable."

In the 1960s, scout officials began a massive campaign to recruit inner-city and backwoods rural boys. Their insight was faultless—scouting could be a lifesaver for at-risk youth—their execution, inept. Rather than rely on the time-tested appeal of the outdoors and of scouting's rules, rituals, and achievements, officials tried to remake scouting into an urban survival program. Rather than call on scouting's long tradition of volunteer service to bring scoutmasters of all colors into the ghetto, they started using CETA funds—that bungling federal work program—to *hire* minority scoutmasters.

Some inner-city troops adopted a veneer of Black Power: one Brooklyn group pledged to ethnic solidarity and black pride, and sported the combat boots, berets, and army fatigues of black radicals. Other troops, however, stuck to the traditional program, to the lasting benefit of their members. "What I picked up was so invaluable," recalls Frederick Simmons, a scout at the Second Canaan Baptist Church in Harlem during the 1960s. "Most of my friends became involved in drugs. Scouting kept me out of trouble." Simmons used to brag to his uncles about his knowledge of knot-tying, chopping wood, and first aid, for these were skills that adults didn't have. He slept with his merit-badge sash wrapped around him. "Every one of those badges represents an achievement; no one gave them to you," he explains. "They helped my self-confidence"—just as Baden-Powell had intended.

And here Simmons touches on the unheralded power of scouting. At a time when government was creating a dependent class, scouting insisted that nothing comes for free. The poorest scout has to pay at least *de minimis* monthly dues; handbooks and uniforms have to be earned, if not paid for in cash, by attendance and gradual progress toward a goal. Merit badges are allocated not on the basis of skin color but according to individual accomplishment.

As for the million-dollar question in scouting—do the scout oath and law actually affect behavior?—Simmons answers an emphatic yes: "I can assure you, we *do* internalize the scouting values," he says. A 1996 Lou Harris study backs Simmons up: men with scouting experience place a higher value on honesty and integrity than men without it.

The 1972 revisions to the scouting program only accelerated the membership decline, and traditional scoutmasters left
the movement in droves. In 1978, scout executives realized
that running after America's convulsive cultural changes was
a losing game: either scouting's founders had discovered
something universal about boys and their attraction to nature
and ritual, or there was little point in existing. So officials
brought mandatory camping skills back into the program, just
in time for the Reagan counterreformation. Membership
started climbing again.

The scouts' commitment to the inner city, however, laud-
ably became permanent. Local scout councils now spend
heavily to recruit minority kids; corporate donations allow
every poor inner-city scout to attend camp. The promise of
scouting—that it is a universal brotherhood blind to class,
race, and religion—has come true. Many scout troops are
wildly diverse, and even all-white troops are an ethnic and religious potpourri.

The inner city has redeemed Baden-Powell's wager that
all kids can respond to the call of the outdoors. The resulting
images are sometimes surreal. In Brooklyn's depressed
Bedford-Stuyvesant neighborhood, ten boys watch a pot-
bellied man in black dress shoes and a scout uniform saw a
log in a church basement. "My thing is, you gotta know the
parts [of the saw]," he throws out to no one in particular.
There are no trees in this stretch of Bedford-Stuyvesant, but
the scouts in Troop 409 pay attention anyway. Neither parents
nor boys see any incongruity. As a Cub Pack skips down Fifth
Avenue singing "America the Beautiful" for the Veterans Day
parade, a single mother tells me that her son is doing a lot of
"interesting things to get ready for the world—camping, tying
knots, building fires. It's very helpful."

Of course, no one today needs to know how to build a fire

97

or pitch a tent. But these skills were always pretextual. Scout-craft teaches, among other things, persistence in the face of disappointment. When it rains and your boots are filled with mud, "you can either take a bad hand and fold, or you can keep playing it, and it will get better," explains Scott Slaton, an Eagle Scout from Atlanta who works with inner-city scouts. In or out of the inner city, this Baden-Powellesque cheerfulness toward adversity is a recipe for success.

Indeed, scouting is a brilliant method for infusing children with a set of values that can be especially hard to find in the inner city. The little details that fill each meeting constantly reinforce a code of conduct based on self-restraint, neatness, and courtesy—the essentials of civilized life. Keeping your uniform in order, standing precisely in line—these are not haphazard naggings. These details define a scout; they are part of his identity. "You guys are the Boy Scouts; you have to set an example for others, so buckle up your lip," a scout-master on West 96th Street barks at his troop before they enter a Cub Scout ceremony. How often do most inner-city teens get to serve as positive role models?

In the most disciplined troops, this search for perfection takes on a sort of magnificence. Henry Lawson, the self-assured leader of Harlem's Troop 759, reminds his troop: "December 18 is my Eagle Scout Court of Honor. Look sharp!" Achieving Eagle Scout status is a rare accomplishment in the ghetto. "Take your uniforms to the cleaner, bring your family, your sister. Look sharp!" he repeats emphatically. "I want *puh-leat-zzz* in your uniforms!" To demonstrate the desired crispness, he delicately pulls his uniform taut at the shoulders with slender fingers. The boys write in their notebooks: "Henry court of honor. Full uniform."

Inner-city boys are starving for discipline; scouting allows them to follow and to lead. Terry, a bucktoothed patrol leader in Brooklyn's Troop 409, leads his troop in a salute and pledge to the flag, after which he announces to his scoutmaster: "Your orders have been carried out, sir." What does this sixteen-year-old most like about scouting? "The sense of giving commands and following orders," he says. "If the scouts don't follow orders, they pay the consequences." Not that it's so easy getting your charges to pay attention. A long-lashed patrol leader sighs sadly about his fractious troop: "I don't know why they are not obeying tonight." If he figures that out, he will be well on his way to assuming leadership as an adult.

The ultimate goal is the fully moral life. In scouting, explains Atlanta's Scott Slaton, "you're surrounded by these ideals. It can be lonely to do the right thing. But if you know it's right, it's right, period, no matter what your friends say." Don't count on children learning that at home or from their peers.

For many ghetto parents, scouting's greatest boon is the scoutmaster. "This is a lifesaver," a single mother tells me. The scoutmaster may be the only stable adult in a child's life. Schools call him about truant boys; single mothers or grandmothers invoke his wrath to try to get a boy to behave. Staten Island's Harvey Johnson exemplifies the male authority figure that inner-city mothers desperately want. "When I take seven to eight boys to camp, I can't accept nothing but discipline," he says. "I'm not a little guy," the burly Johnson explains slyly. "Now, that boy isn't absolutely certain that I won't get real mad; he can't swear it. He's thinking: 'I don't know if he'll kill me or not,'" Johnson chuckles, "'so I better do what he wants.'" Johnson is fiercely dedicated to scouting's values and to bringing boys into their orbit. "Scouting is corny," he says proudly. "You try to sell that corniness to the boys: that it's all right to salute the flag and respect your family." Black kids don't need the militancy of the 1960s anymore, he says—not at this stage of history. "You have to know how to build a fire and pitch a tent," he asserts. "I can't do that and walk around with my fist in the air." Johnson strives to spread scouting's values to a scout's parents, too, in an ever-widening circle of influence. He tries to teach mothers that their every gesture is a moral example—for better or worse—to their boys, and to persuade fathers, if they are around, to take responsibility for their children.

Unfortunately, men like Johnson are hard to find in the inner city. Scout councils have continued paying scoutmasters in areas where they can find no volunteers; the New York Council even hires former welfare recipients, a practice other councils rightly frown upon. Local councils today ought to cast a far wider net to find men, regardless of color, willing to help poor boys. They should send out a call to New York's civic-minded corporations that they need men for a proven program for guiding boys into adulthood. These companies, which already finance camperships and provide tutors and mentors for a wide range of youth activities, are sure to respond.

The traditional values of scouting are shriveling up everywhere today; in troubled neighborhoods, they are a precious balm. "When I see my neighbors carrying bags, I'm supposed to help them automatically," announces Dayshon Green, a round twelve-year-old scout in Bedford-Stuyvesant. "You're supposed to tell the truth; the truth will set you free."

I have seen tiny civilities in scout meetings across New York that may have been common seventy-five years ago but that today make the heart rejoice. As a Cub Pack meeting near Columbia University is drawing to a close, one of its young leaders, a vivacious Peruvian-American named Thomas, pauses to consider his options. "And now we're going to . . .

to . . ." His inspiration arrives: ". . . sing a song for our guest!" And the boys break out into a lusty rendition of the "Cub Scout Spirit" for me, complete with body spins. At the conclusion of the Troop 409 meeting in Bedford-Stuyvesant, the boys thank me in unison for coming. Two fawn-like boys at a meeting on the Lower East Side politely introduce themselves, offering their hands. When I ask one of them, Ian, where he got his good manners, he clutches his handbook to his chest and says, "I've practically memorized my Boy Scout book." The handbook says nothing about introducing yourself to adults; apparently its civilizing influence is wider than its literal words.

Scouting is taking up the schools' slack regarding American history and government, too. At a merit badge rally last November (a "teach-in" for merit badges), a dumpling-shaped lady in a scout uniform grilled boys in large parkas about American government. "Fellows, if we don't know our Declaration of Independence, our Preamble, and our Constitution, we don't know anything about our nation," she chastised them in a heavy Queens accent. "Does anyone know the first three words of the Preamble?" At a time when 25 percent of college seniors in a recent poll thought that the Marxist maxim "From each according to his abilities, to each according to his needs," was a Constitutional phrase, the scouts' emphasis on civics is crucial. "There are very few activities that allow you to get into a traditional form of American education," a single mother of a Cub Scout told me. "You need some fundamentals and basics."

The scouts are probably kids' only source of basic training in patriotism today. Cultivating a love of country in disadvantaged boys is a cure for alienation; it centers them in an identity far larger and more valuable than race or class and assures them that this is *their* country, too. Thomas, the radiant

Peruvian-American Cub leader, tried to teach tiny Wolf Cubs about the flag last November. "Okay, the first thing we need to talk about is the Pledge of Allegiance," he announced enthusiastically. "Who knows what it means? What is allegiance?" The boys stare fascinated at Thomas, with open mouths and huge eyes. No response. He cheerfully continues his one-sided Socratic dialogue. "Allegiance is to respect our country. Allegiance is to be true. Who knows what a republic is? It's our kind of government. Do you learn about history in school?" All the boys shake their heads no. Thomas then hits unwittingly on the essential paradox of ordered liberty: "Liberty is freedom for you and others," he explains. "We're all free to do what we want. Except," he reflects judiciously, ". . . well, rules."

The scouts have recovered their 1970s membership losses and are now growing at a fast clip, especially in the suburbs, as many parents increasingly realize that they can't raise decent children in a value-free environment. Even so, the elites in the press, the universities, and the chattering professions, having thoroughly absorbed the adversarial values of the 1960s, have kept the scouts from regaining their place in the American imagination. Nothing could be more repugnant to elite values than the scouts, with their traditional manliness, as two revisionist histories from the early 1980s make clear. In *Building Character in the American Boy: The Boy Scouts, the YMCA, and Their Forerunners: 1870–1920*, historian David Macleod portrays that era's effort to inculcate honor and duty in boys as merely the hysterical reaction of a neurotic upper class to adolescent sexuality. Noting with derision the scouts' emphasis on sexual abstinence till marriage, Macleod sneers that "pleasure of course never skulked across the stage." Presumably, because scout leaders did not discuss, say, masturbation or orgasm or condom etiquette, as do today's sex educators, they betrayed their charges. Forget duty to others;

today's academy teaches that only the self and all its polymorphous desires counts.

Macleod scoffs at the wide-ranging knowledge of American history and government the early scouts acquired. Where, he bleats, is the scouts' call for "critical thinking on how to effect political change"? Like all contemporary advocates of "critical thinking," Macleod forgets that you can't think until you know something, and like most radical profs, he takes for granted that any critical thinker will call for a new political system.

In the same vein, Columbia English professor Michael Rosenthal presents scouting as a terrified upper-class effort at social control; he indulges in much self-righteous chest-thumping about the evils of imperialism as well. Baden-Powell designed scouting, he argues in *The Character Factory: Baden-Powell's Boy Scouts and the Imperatives of Empire*, to create docile automata who would mindlessly perform the duties of empire. Rosenthal astoundingly sees in the inspiring scout law, with its supreme emphasis on selflessness and kindness to others, "one quality only—obedience." Echoing Macleod's knee-jerk call for "critical thinking," he reduces scouting to "hatred of dissent [and] fear of the independent critical mind"—which, of course, will think only approved sixties thoughts.

Since the 1960s, academia has trumpeted itself as a selfless, public-spirited counterweight to greedy, materialistic America. But that's an empty claim compared to scouting's full-throated championship of chivalric duty and its opposition to the selfish individualism of industrial society. Faced with the call to help others *"before everything else,"* in Baden-Powell's words—before, that is, all the imperatives of the self—the modern academic shrivels up, reaches for his *latte*, and whines about "critical thinking."

Just as the academic debunkers began to hyperventilate,

the American litigation machine started to gear up against the scouts. The organization has always had its share of critics, charging the scouts variously with being too pacifist, too militarist, too capitalist, or too internationalist. In the 1920s, for example, the secretary of the Young Communist League warned Baden-Powell to expect a fight to the finish. Baden-Powell lightly stepped aside: "You can't fight without two," he replied calmly. "Our aim is to help the poorer boy, independent of all political questions, to get his fair chance of happiness and success in life."

But unlike early critics, who often simply went and formed alternative organizations, today's opponents have been suing to get into the scouts and dismantle it from within. Atheist Elliot Welsh of Burr Ridge, Illinois, is a typical scout litigant. He characterized the Tiger Cub Promise, "I promise to love God, my family, and my country, and to learn about the world," as "bigoted, outmoded boilerplate." Did he send his six-year-old son Mark to an American Atheist camp instead? Of course not. He sued the scouts in 1989 for violating his son's rights. As an alleged "public accommodation," Welsh argued, the scouts could not ask their members to declare reverence for God.

Girls, atheists, and homosexuals have all sued the scouts. Until recently, the scouts always won, on the grounds that they were a private entity, not a "public accommodation" like a restaurant or a hotel. As such, they should be allowed to set their own membership and leadership criteria, consonant with their moral purpose. Nevertheless, the litigation has been a public-relations nightmare. The press, of course, ate up every challenge, while ignoring the daily good that the scouts perform. When Timothy Curran, a homosexual Eagle Scout, lost his bid to become a Berkeley, California, scoutmaster—he reportedly wanted to teach kids that there was nothing wrong with the homosexual life—Bay Area institutions sprang into action. Levi Strauss, Wells Fargo, the United Way of San Francisco, and the Bank of America stopped funding the scouts (the Bank of America subsequently restored funding); San Francisco and Oakland schools banned school-day scout programs. Companies elsewhere are joining the bandwagon: in a paroxysm of self-righteousness, Fleet Bank of Providence criticized the scouts for their ban on avowed homosexual scoutmasters while publicly accepting a scout award.

For those scout funders and sponsoring institutions that have withdrawn their support, it comes down to this: furthering the gay-rights crusade takes precedence over helping inner-city children—all the lost funding was earmarked for inner-city scouting or training for minority scoutmasters. New York state senator Tom Duane and Queens schoolteacher Danny Drum, both homosexual activists, are pressing the New York City Board of Education to end their support of scouting camperships for poor children. "I don't think students should go to a camp like that, whose organizers clearly discriminate against gays and lesbians," Drum explained. I asked him whether the young campers were even aware of the scouts' views on homosexuality. No, he answered: "The fact that [homosexuality] is not talked about is one of the biggest problems."

Ironically, the scouts' reticence about homosexuality is what finally ended its winning streak in the courts. Last August, the New Jersey Supreme Court ordered the scouts to reinstate James Dale as a scoutmaster, despite his public homosexual-rights activism. Not only did the Court find that the scouts were a "place" of "public accommodation," akin to a business establishment, but it concluded that the scouts have no First Amendment right to select leaders committed to their chosen moral message.

The Court rejected the scouts' First Amendment defense on several grounds: that fighting discrimination against homosexuals is supremely important; that having a homosexual scout leader is really no big deal; and that finally, though the scouts claim to believe that open homosexuality undermines their family-values message, they don't really mean it. The Court reached this astounding conclusion thus: since the scouts don't rant about homosexuality, since in fact they are virtually silent on the matter in their published materials, and since *as we all know* there is nothing more benighted than disapproving of homosexual conduct, the scouts misinterpret their own moral oath. The scouts may claim that their injunction to keep "morally straight" proscribes homosexual conduct, but they're wrong. The Court knows better.

If the New Jersey *Dale* decision stands, you can say goodbye to an independent private sphere. If the government can tell private, values-based groups what they *really* believe, free thought will go underground. If private groups have no freedom to choose their own leaders, private groups will wither away. What better way to destroy the scouts than to force on them leaders opposed to their core convictions? James Dale feels obliged to "point out" to scout administrators "how bad and wrong" their stance against homosexual conduct is; given the compulsively proselytizing character of the homosexual-rights movement, some homosexual-activist scoutmasters will inevitably also "point out" to the boys themselves their right to choose a homosexual life over a heterosexual family.

The New Jersey Supreme Court breezily declared that forcing homosexual scoutmasters on the scouts would have no effect on the organization. Seasoned scoutmasters know better. Francis Harty, a veteran Staten Island scoutmaster who has helped dozens of boys become Eagle Scouts, says: "I have no problem with a gay person in scouting. I'd have a hell of a time telling parents he's taking their boys into the woods." People will leave in "droves," predicts Baltimore scoutmaster Harry Shaw. "And we thought it was bad in the 1970s."

The Scout litigation is an alarm that America's obsession with alleged discrimination has gone too far. Elite culture now sees the highest function of government as correcting the petty prejudices of the citizens, even if that means destroying civil society in the process. If the government's crusade against so-called bigotry means eviscerating the scouts, it is long past time to shut the crusade down. Scouting does more good in a year than an army of ACLU lawyers has ever done. Although scouting has been battered by time, although its top officials are public-relations incompetents, it remains the paramount character-education program of our era, as a host of copycat programs such as Outward Bound testify. Everyone who cares about poor children—everyone who cares about teaching values to boys—should embrace it wholeheartedly and rally to its defense.

[2000]

BRIAN C. ANDERSON

How Catholic Charities
Lost Its Soul

AS ADVANCED SOCIAL THINKERS rediscover the power of
faith-based institutions to rescue the down-and-out by transforming the dysfunctional worldview that often lies at the root
of their difficulties, you would think that Catholic Charities
USA would be a perfect model to emulate, getting the poor
into the mainstream by emphasizing moral values and ethical
conduct. But no: rather than trying to promote traditional values and God-fearing behavior, Catholic Charities—and the
same could be said about the Association of Jewish Family
and Children's Agencies or the Lutheran Services in America—has become over the last three decades an arm of the welfare state, with 65 percent of its $2.3 billion annual budget
now flowing from government sources and little that is explic-

itly religious, or even values-laden, about most of the services its 1,400 member agencies and 46,000 paid employees provide.

Far from being a model for reforming today's welfare-state approach to helping the poor, Catholic Charities USA is one of the nation's most powerful advocates for outworn welfare-state ideas, especially the idea that social and economic forces over which the individual has no control, rather than his own attitudes and behavior, are the reason for poverty. The example of this multibillion-dollar charity should serve as a warning to policy makers seeking to privatize the care of the needy that they had better pick and choose prudently: for some of the institutions of civil society have been tainted with the same value-free worldview that has made most government-run poverty efforts a hindrance rather than a help to the poor.

Until the 1960s, Catholic charitable institutions—benevolent societies, hospitals, orphanages, reformatories, and the like—did exemplary work, serving the poor and bringing them into the mainstream of American life. In New York, the tireless philanthropic efforts of Catholic leaders like Archbishop John Hughes during the second half of the nineteenth century so uplifted Gotham's immigrant Irish—at the time America's first underclass—that by the turn of the twentieth century most of them were mainstream American citizens. (See "How Dagger John Saved New York's Irish.")

Hughes recognized that, though some of the poor were victims of circumstance, many were poor because of self-destructive behavior—sinful behavior, as he had no hesitation in calling it. The goal of charity to such people was to change their values and beliefs. And what was more powerful in working such a transformation than religion? It gives the needy a set of authoritative dos and don'ts, stresses the importance of personal responsibility and the overcoming of per-

109

sonal failings, offers membership in a meaning-rich community, requires responsibility to family, and forgives past transgressions if one makes a fresh start.

This vigorously moral approach guided Catholic Charities from its formal inception in 1910, as the records of its yearly meetings make clear. Edwin J. Cooley, a former chief of Catholic Charities' New York City probation bureau, is representative; speaking to the organization's 1926 annual conference, he stressed that juvenile crime sprang from bad habits and dysfunctional values, and that the best way to solve it was to remake those habits and values through religious faith and moral instruction. Though after World War II, a stress on government's responsibility to provide relief to the poor grows louder, and one hears lots more psychological and sociological jargon, talk of "virtue," "character," and "rooting out vice" still dominates the organization's annual proceedings.

But the understanding of poverty as often inseparable from moral and cultural considerations disintegrated in the late 1960s. Swept up in the decade's tumult and encouraged by the modernizing spirit of the second Vatican Council, Catholic Charities rejected its long-standing emphasis on personal responsibility and self-reliance and began to blame capitalist society rather than individual behavior for poverty and crime. It now looked to the welfare state to solve all social problems. Today, through a continual whirlwind of policy statements and lobbying, and by fostering countless activist community organizations, Catholic Charities has become, as Richard John Neuhaus, a priest and editor of the esteemed religious journal *First Things*, puts it, "a chief apologist for a catastrophically destructive welfare system, and it stands in the way of developing alternatives to help people break out of dependency and take charge of their lives."

Catholic Charities first announced its politicization in a

wild-eyed manifesto that invokes such radical sixties icons as Malcolm X, Gloria Steinem, Herbert Marcuse, and—above all—the Marxist-inspired Liberation Theology movement that (to put it crudely) equates Jesus with Che Guevara. Ratified at Catholic Charities' annual meeting in 1972, the so-called Cadre Study totally abandoned any stress on personal responsibility in relation to poverty and other social ills. Instead, it painted America as an unjust, "numb" country, whose oppressive society and closed economy cause people to turn to crime or drugs or prostitution. Moreover, the study asserts, individual acts of charity are useless. We must instead unearth "the root causes of poverty and oppression" and radically reconstruct—"humanize and transform"—the social order to avert social upheaval.

This radical shift in thinking had two practical consequences. First, Catholic Charities moved away from "just" charity toward a stress on government solutions to every social problem, making political advocacy a key mission. "We undertook to get more involved in making a contribution to the formation of public policy," says former Catholic Charities president Monsignor Lawrence Corcoran, one of the authors of the Cadre Study. Second, Catholic Charities began to organize local communities to resist "unjust" social structures. As Corcoran delicately puts it, "We also increased our activities in the field of social action, over and above the traditional role of charity."

At the same time, as the War on Poverty got under way, the federal government increasingly contracted with Catholic Charities agencies to provide welfare services. Those agencies, imbued with their new faith in government's potential to solve social problems, eagerly accepted government money. Catholic Charities received nearly a quarter of its funding from government by the end of the sixties, over half by the

111

late seventies, and more than 60 percent by the mid-eighties, where it has remained ever since. As they became government contractors, the agencies began to serve more non-Catholics and to hire non-Catholics too, usually professional social workers with ardent faith in the welfare state.

Under its pugnacious current president, Jesuit Fred Kammer, a lawyer (who attended Yale Law with Bill Clinton) and author of *Doing Faithjustice*, a widely used textbook that gives a leftist twist to Catholic social thought, the organization has expanded and professionalized its advocacy work. The forty-member central headquarters in Alexandria, Virginia, assembles a legislative agenda, lobbies Congress and the White House, and, through weekly "Advofaxes," alerts member agencies and subscribers to impending federal and state legislation on social policy. But as Marvin Olasky, author of *The Tragedy of American Compassion*, an influential book on charity, remarks, "This isn't charity at all. When you take away dollars that you could spend helping people and spend them on lobbying, you're robbing the poor to give to the lobbyist."

Worse still, the policies that Catholic Charities advocates in its lobbying activities also hurt, rather than help, the poor. Take four examples. First, Catholic Charities was the nation's loudest opponent of the 1996 welfare-reform law, lobbying hard on Capitol Hill and meeting with the president to derail it. Kammer prophesied that the new law would be "a national social catastrophe.... No one will be spared the consequences." But today, with the welfare rolls plummeting 50 percent in just three years and anecdotal evidence suggesting that many former recipients are happy to be liberated from dependency and in control of their own lives, Kammer's dire predictions seem ludicrous.

Second, Catholic Charities has lobbied to boost the minimum wage above $6 from the current $5.15. Most reputable economists point out, however, that such a hike would cost the nation hundreds of thousands of entry-level jobs, hurting just the people—immigrants, inner-city youths, or former welfare recipients rejoining the workforce—whom Catholic Charities says it cares most about. Catholic Charities seems not to grasp that minimum-wage positions are usually first jobs—most minimum-wage earners are teens, and only 2.8 percent of minimum-wage earners are over thirty.

Third, Catholic Charities vociferously opposes the privatization of Social Security. In 1998, Kammer's deputy for public policy, Sharon Daly, shared a podium with Jesse Jackson, Patricia Ireland of the National Organization of Women, NAACP head Kweisi Mfume, and John Sweeney of the AFL-CIO—a rainbow coalition of prominent leftists—to denounce the idea. Asks Cato Institute tax specialist Stephen Moore, why would an organization dedicated to helping "the poorest among us," as Catholic Charities' motto goes, urge Congress to reject a proposal allowing the poor to opt out of a system that offers them a dismal return on their tax dollars? Private retirement accounts, Moore argues, would give those few individuals making the minimum wage for their entire lives a retirement income 50 percent to 100 percent higher than what Social Security promises. Given this evidence, Moore ruminates, the opposition to private accounts must be ideological: "Some people are simply predisposed to favor big government," he sighs.

Finally, Catholic Charities tirelessly argues that racism "is a root cause of the economic and social oppression in our society," as "Vision 2000," a key recent policy paper, asserts. Speaking to me in his cluttered Alexandria office, Kammer explains: "Race remains at the heart of the social question in America—and as a southerner, I *really* believe that." He has installed a trendy "diversity officer" at the national headquarters to keep race front and center in the organization's activities.

113

This unrealistic view of race distorts the whole organization's thinking about black crime. Catholic Charities lobbies hard in favor of requirements that force states to provide detailed explanations for why so many blacks are behind bars—the presumption being that racism is to blame. Catholic Charities believes that if black ten- to seventeen-year-olds are only 15 percent of the population but 26 percent of all juveniles arrested and 46 percent of all juveniles doing time, this is *prima facie* evidence of racism. But if black youths have, as they do, a far higher rate of criminal activity than white kids, why would anyone expect them not to be arrested and convicted at a higher rate?

At bottom, Catholic Charities appears to suspect that, for black kids, crime is somehow justified. Kammer, writing in 1996, asserts, "If young men turn to crack and crime because there are no jobs and no hopes, then you and I become addicted with them." In other words, in an unjust, racist society, poor kids have no recourse but to rob and do dope. But doesn't this only justify thuggery and self-destruction, exactly the message inner-city kids don't need to hear?

Following the lead of the central office, some 90 percent of Catholic Charities' local agencies lobby in state legislatures. Patrick Johnson, director of Hartford, Connecticut's Catholic Charities agency, enthuses: "We have one of the largest social-justice advocacy programs in the country, with a lobbyist on staff, actively lobbying the state legislature in the area of welfare reform, against the death penalty, juvenile justice—the social-services agenda, if you will." As Johnson, a prominent member of Catholic Charities' national board, sums up, "Charity is never enough; you have to do other stuff."

The "other stuff" includes "parish social ministry," the second big thrust of today's Catholic Charities. In part, parish social ministry just means spurring the members of local parishes to do traditional, and effective, good works: to visit the elderly, say, or take care of neighborhood kids. But, troublingly, it also means politically oriented community organizing. As one disgruntled local Catholic Charities representative explains, this means encouraging low-income parishioners to form "agitation networks" to lobby politicians, stage protests, and pursue "social change" by demanding more entitlements from the welfare state or by intimidating a local utility into adopting a no shutoff policy when bills aren't paid.

These community organizing efforts use as their textbook one of the classics of extreme left-wing literature—Saul Alinsky's 1947 *Reveille for Radicals*. In Alinsky's far-left vision, promoted by his quasi-Marxist Industrial Areas Foundation, the organizer aims to get his followers to accumulate power for militant ends. Explains Tom Ulrich, the Catholic Charities' national director of "Training and Convening," which instructs local personnel in parish social ministry, "To bring people together to create a power base so that they can influence their local communities—that's important in parish social ministry, and very much influenced by Alinsky and the IAF." Ulrich never asks, however, whether getting low-income people to agitate for social change, rather than helping them to get their lives in order to take advantage of the opportunities multiplying around them, is the most effective way to liberate the poor.

If Catholic Charities' lobbying and community organizing don't help the poor, what about the third and largest area of its activities, the array of services that local agencies provide? Here, it's hard to be categorical: the agencies serve over ten million people with a staggering number of individual problems, and some agencies and programs are atypical, like the robustly faith-filled Tulsa Catholic Charities, which accepts no government funds. Making judgment harder, Catholic Charities agencies don't focus on the outcomes of

115

their activities, so nobody knows what they're accomplishing. An otherwise no-nonsense nun running a Catholic Charities educational program for at-risk youth in Queens is typical. She struggles to impart self-esteem—despite the evidence that shows at-risk kids have self-esteem to spare—and she has no clue what happens as a result of her efforts. "I just don't have the resources," she complains.

Kathleen McGowan, head of Catholic Charities' national board, notes that her organization has "started to address this problem, absolutely." But as Gary MacDougal, a trustee of the left-leaning Annie E. Casey Foundation, succinctly observes, "There's little point in offering more services if their long-term effectiveness is unclear."

The teeming array of Catholic Charities services fall into two broad categories. The first, emergency services, includes food-assistance programs, such as soup kitchens, feeding more than 4 million people, and temporary shelter, offering 2.8 million nights of shelter in 1997. Disaster relief, clothing assistance, help in paying overdue utilities bills—you name the emergency, Catholic Charities helps out.

The second category, social services, provides child care, legal and employment services, AIDS hospices, and so on to almost 1 million people, as well as such educational programs as English as a second language courses and Head Start programs. The organization's vast world of social services also includes counseling, neighborhood-based programs like Big Brothers and senior centers, refugee resettlement, health care, housing, and adoption.

Government pays for most of this activity, and with government funds come restrictions. Charities must follow time-wasting rules that reduce flexibility and require a one-size-fits-all approach to treating people with endlessly various problems.

Worse, until recently the regulations have prohibited charities from including a strong religious dimension in their programs. For wayward kids, for welfare moms trying to break free of dependency, for heroin addicts or drunks trying to kick the habit, faith-based programs work best. Psychologist David Larson at the National Institute for Healthcare Research cites many studies that show a strong correlation between religious participation and rejecting crime and substance abuse; criminologist Byron Johnson of Lamar University has shown big drops in recidivism for prisoners who go through Charles Colson's faith-based Prison Fellowship Program.

Catholic Charities would have found none of this surprising seventy years ago, but many of today's Catholic Charities agencies pay little attention to the power of faith to transform lives. Pennsylvania Senator Rick Santorum sparked a fierce controversy in 1996 when he rebuked Catholic Charities for drifting away from the faith under the pressure of government funding. Santorum told of a priest he knows who began a psychology internship at a Catholic Charities clinic. The clinic supervisor tested him on three hypothetical counseling situations: a depressed pregnant woman who wants to abort her child, two homosexuals seeking advice on their relationship, and a divorcing couple asking for counseling. In keeping with Catholic teachings, the priest advised against the abortion, refused to endorse homosexual unions, and encouraged the divorcing couple to save their marriage. He failed the test. His supervisor explained: "We get government funds, so we are not Catholic."

Such cases abound. Catholic Charities in Albany, New York, has proposed starting a health maintenance organization that would make abortion referrals; Catholic Charities in San Francisco, to keep its city contracts, now complies

117

with the local law extending spousal benefits to unmarried heterosexuals and homosexual live-in partners; Catholic Charities in Oakland, California, recently ran programs that encourage public school social-science instructors to discuss in a favorable light "same-sex marriage," "gays in the military," and "family diversity" starting in the first grade. In a wide-ranging survey of nonprofit religious charities, sociologist Stephen Monsma found that a third of Catholic child-care agencies had felt government pressure to curtail their religious practices. For policy makers, the issue is not how Catholic or anti-Catholic such measures may be, but rather how much they separate Catholic Charities from the values that once made the organization distinct from—and more effective than—an off-the-shelf welfare-state approach to the poor.

A further powerful secularizing force on Catholic Charities is the New York–based Council on Accreditation of Services for Families and Children. "With the government money, accrediting became essential," one worried official of Catholic Charities observes, "but the stress with COA is political and secular—on diversity, consumer advocacy, lobbying for more government funds, organizing for change in the community—all these things you have to do to keep your accreditation up." The Council now accredits twelve hundred welfare-services providers, mental health services, consumer credit counselors—and a growing number of Catholic Charities agencies. Says Kathleen McGowan, chair of Catholic Charities' national board: "Most of us feel that it is of value to have that kind of accreditation for agencies—it tells the community and our benefactors that we meet a national set of standards." But the standards of the failed welfare state?

I spent a day visiting Catholic Charities' programs in some of New York's poorest neighborhoods with Communications Director Margaret Keaveney of the Brooklyn and Queens agency, and I came back with mixed impressions. Keaveney, a fount of good sense, stressed the importance of the agency's Catholic identity in what they do, but none of what I saw seemed explicitly religious in spirit.

On the admirable end of the scale, the city-funded Peter J. Dellamonica Center for Seniors in Queens bustles with old folks painting, playing cards, sitting down to a snack together, or participating in seminars on quality-of-life themes for the elderly. Equally admirable was an apartment building in Brooklyn, which Catholic Charities, with city money, transformed from a roach-infested crack house into a reduced-rent apartment building with strict rules of civility for low-income families.

But a program that brings food to the homeless and tries to connect them to government services and to Alcoholics and Narcotics Anonymous was less impressive. One outreach worker, exuding righteous anger, passionately attacked welfare reform and absurdly claimed that most of her clients "work" nine-to-five jobs because they recycle bottles and cans. "Nobody says to the homeless: 'I don't mind the smell of urine and feces, let me hear what the issue is in your life,'" she lamented. One homeless man we met, "Cornbread," eloquently denounced the Giuliani administration and offered his solution to the homeless problem: "Take all the abandoned buildings in New York and give them to the homeless to run," he urged. As an outreach worker gushed agreement, Keaveney quickly interjected that such a proposal would be unrealistic, since most of the homeless are mentally ill, substance abusers, or both. If ever lost souls needed salvation, it's Cornbread and his neighbors; yet salvation is one thing that Catholic Charities' secularized program doesn't provide.

Two contrasting programs for unwed mothers make clear

how dramatically a moral, faith-based message can improve the lives of the poor. An all-too-typical program in Brooklyn I visited hooks up young, pregnant women to public services, wrestles with their housing problems, and tries to prepare them for motherhood. Everything the program does—including surrounding the office with stuffed animals—conveys the idea that having illegitimate kids is just an accepted part of the community's life. But since many of these young women will be chronically poor, and their children are likely to have a high rate of social failure, the program, which has little to say about morality, sends exactly the wrong signals.

Very different is Sister Connie Driscoll's celebrated St. Martin de Porres House of Hope in Chicago's blighted Woodlawn neighborhood. Since 1983, Driscoll has provided shelter and counsel to more than eleven thousand homeless women, many with illegitimate kids and most of them substance abusers when they first come to her. Driscoll takes no government money, to avoid having to tone down her moral message of responsibility and work. She puts her charges to work around the house from the moment they arrive to start building the message that they're responsible for their own fate. Their days are filled with Alcoholics and Narcotics Anonymous meetings, GED classes, computer training, and constant moral instruction on the dangers of illegitimacy and irresponsible sexual behavior. No men may visit. If the young women don't follow her rules, she kicks them out. "We feel that if people aren't willing to help themselves take a step forward and become responsible for their own actions," she informs me, "there's not much we can do to help them." Though Driscoll doesn't directly evangelize—"our purpose is to allow people to see the faith that moves us, and let it guide their lives," she says—her House of Hope is in every way an exemplary Catholic charity. Her success speaks for itself: almost all the women overcome their addictions; only 5 percent return to shelters.

Catholicism's traditional social doctrine doesn't look much like the big-government line that Catholic Charities espouses. To be sure, there's a radical, politicized tradition in the Church, running from the revolutionary millennialism of five hundred years ago to the French "worker priests" and the liberation theologians of the twentieth century. But orthodox Catholic social teaching is based on a deeply realistic understanding of man's nature as fallen. For two millennia, the Church has taught that man has a hardwired inclination to sin that, unchecked, leads to drunkenness, envy, lust, selfishness, and a host of other sins. Such a disordered life undermines community and leads to self-destruction. But Catholic doctrine also holds that man possesses the freedom, with the help of God's grace, to master unruly passions and follow the moral teachings of the Church, beginning with the Ten Commandments, and so to live a life of inner peace in responsible community with other men. It is this unambiguous moral inheritance—a time-tested recipe for reducing poverty and other social ills as well as nurturing fulfilled lives—that Catholic Charities today has lost sight of in its turn to the state as the primary solution for society's pathologies.

In recent years, Catholic thinkers have focused on the kind of society that best fosters moral development. They have stressed the idea of "subsidiarity," by which they mean that "higher" or larger associations should help "lower," smaller associations but not replace or inhibit them except when they no longer function. In other words, the state should not displace the responsibilities of the family or the neighborhood but should try to strengthen these entities so that they can fulfill their appropriate duties. Thus, responsibility for social and moral life, subsidiarity holds, resides first with the individual, and then, in ascending order, with those closest to him: family, friends, neighborhood, local government, and— only as a last resort, after other levels have failed—the state. But Catholic Charities is openly unenthusiastic about subsidiarity. "There has been a lot of romantic nonsense lately in Washington," Kammer grumbled a little while back, "to the effect that state and local governments are always more effective and efficient than the national government. The [false] claim is that local people know best." As for holding individuals responsible for their plight—suggesting, for example, that welfare mothers shouldn't have gotten pregnant out of wedlock—Kammer bristles. "I don't buy the argument that it's moral turpitude," he says.

Catholic Charities also ignores Pope John Paul II's warnings about the dangers of the "Social Assistance State," the welfare system that proliferates upon the ruins of subsidiarity. By "intervening directly" and robbing "society of its responsibility," the pope warns in a 1991 encyclical, the Social Assistance State "leads to a loss of human energies" and multiplies public agencies that treat people like numbers and squander money to no good end.

According to Bishop Joseph Sullivan, a writer of the Cadre Study and today liaison between Catholic Charities and the U.S. Catholic Bishops, the pope didn't have the U.S. in mind in his criticisms of the Social Assistance State. "While a lot of people might think that there's enough social welfare or socialism in the United States," the bishop tells me, we in fact need more, not less, government. "I think we've got a long way to go, especially when a CEO makes 419 times what the average factory worker makes," Sullivan adds, with Catholic Charities' characteristic stress on the inequality of American society.

As both leading presidential candidates, Vice President

Gore and Governor Bush, seek to extend "Charitable Choice," the provision of the 1996 federal welfare-reform law that allows faith-based institutions to receive government funding to serve the needy without veiling their religious character, some conservative critics worry that government funds might make other faith-based institutions more like Catholic Charities—more secular and less concerned with saving souls. But this argument assumes that it was government funding that corrupted Catholic Charities. In fact, Catholic Charities officials already sincerely believed that government entitlements are the best way to help the needy when they began accepting government funding. There's no reason to think that effective faith-based institutions, once receiving government money under charitable choice, would lose their way. As Richard John Neuhaus has argued, it's up to those who run faith-based programs to ensure that they preserve their religious integrity under charitable choice. "There are millions of people, especially the poor," Neuhaus says, "who would greatly benefit by programs aimed not simply at 'delivering services' but at transforming lives."

As for Catholic Charities itself, unless it changes its vision—embracing subsidiarity, following examples like Sister Connie Driscoll's, and abandoning its illusion that America is an unjust and racist country—charitable choice won't make a bit of difference for it, or for those it serves.

[2000]

123

HEATHER MAC DONALD

Behind the Hundred
Neediest Cases

ON DECEMBER 15, 1912, the *New York Times* ran a highly unorthodox headline: SANTA CLAUS PLEASE TAKE NOTICE! HERE ARE
NEW YORK'S 100 NEEDIEST CASES. The equally unorthodox story
began: "Fathoms deep beneath the exhilaration and joyous-
ness of Christmas there is a world of desolation and hunger
which few of the dwellers in light and air have had time or
chance to realize; the world of famine in the midst of plenty, of
cruel heart and body hunger with bounty in sight, but not in
reach." There followed one hundred short case histories of
what the *Times* called the "uttermost dregs of the city's poor,"
culled from the files of the city's three largest charity organizations.

The response was immediate: food, blankets, toys, and

124

clothing poured into the *Times*'s offices, along with offers of adoption, employment, and medical care. The "Hundred Neediest Cases" appeal became an instant Christmas tradition, growing exponentially from its first $3,630.88 to reach nearly $5 million annually today.

Behind this growth lies a profound change, however. The prototypical needy case in the first decades of the appeal was a struggling widow or plucky orphan; today's is more likely to be a single mother of five who finds her welfare check inadequate. This change reflects one of the century's most momentous cultural developments: the transformation of elite opinion regarding poverty and need. The elite once held the poor to the same standards of behavior that it set for itself: moral character determined the strength of a person's claim for assistance. Those who worked and struggled and yet were overwhelmed by adversity deserved help; the idle and dissolute did not. Over time, though, elite opinion came to see the cause of poverty not in individual character and behavior but in vast, impersonal social and economic forces that supposedly determined individual fate. In response, need became the sole criterion for aid, with moral character all but irrelevant. The Neediest Cases appeal concludes this century an agnostic regarding individual responsibility and a strident advocate of the welfare state. The story of how it got there traces the rise of moral relativism among opinion and policy makers, the triumph of the entitlement ethos, and the transformation of the *New York Times* itself into a proponent of victimology and double standards.

At the heart of the first Neediest Cases appeals lay a crucial moral distinction between the deserving and the undeserving poor. *Times* publisher Adolph Ochs started the appeal to channel the charitable impulse of the Christmas season toward the truly needy, as certified by the charity organizations that distributed the donations. Those who tried to make a career out of poverty or refused to help themselves would not get aid. Unapologetic about its moral approach, the *Times* opened its 1913 appeal with this admonition: "Because the Christmas spirit is strong within you, do not give to the professional beggars on the streets, unworthy, all of them, and often criminals." Such "indiscriminate giving" only encouraged pauperism. The *Times* proposed to educate readers into a deeper understanding of poverty.

The distinction between the deserving and undeserving poor was particularly relevant to early twentieth-century New York. It was a world where upright individuals could work extraordinarily hard—as factory hands, seamstresses, and laundresses—and still be poor. Misfortune was everywhere. Tuberculosis and other diseases crippled or killed entire families. Mental illness sent children and adults alike to "institutions." Most important, no government safety net existed; private charity was the sole external resource available to the poor.

The first case histories reflected these hard realities, with tuberculosis, in particular, a leitmotif. What is most striking about the articles is their moral fervor, often shading into sentimentality. They made strong emotional appeals, emphasizing family values and individual courage. A case headlined YOUNG WIFE'S CHEERLESS FUTURE from 1913 is typical in accentuating the pathos of its subject: "In a large department store a pale, toil-worn woman stands all day behind the glove counter. Despite her cheerless life and an apparently hopeless future, she is always courteous to customers, patient and obliging. Her husband is in a hospital, an advanced case of tuberculosis. There are three delicate children at school." The young wife is on the verge of a physical collapse, her wages insufficient to pay the rent and provide food. The article asks for assistance until thirteen-year-old Katherine, the eldest of the children, is "ready to help."

Case 92 from 1912 struck another familiar theme—the orphan "little mother": "A girl of nineteen is being father and mother both to a cluster of little brothers and sisters, six in number, and her next youngest brother, now sixteen, is helping her as much as he can. She spends her days in a shop and her nights at home as a cook, dressmaker, and nurse to her little family." Such stories were lessons in the virtues of perseverance and responsibility.

Widows also dominated the first decades of the appeal, their plight described with unabashed emotionalism. A twenty-year-old widow from 1912, for example, too frail from childbirth to support herself, is "resisting with all her might and main the impulse to send her child to an institution because it is the one beautiful and wonderful thing left to her of her starved and chilled romance." This emphasis on the innocence and worthiness of the charity recipients prevailed for the next four decades.

Throughout the twenties the *Times* held firmly to its moralized view of poverty and asserted the rectitude and purity of its beneficiaries, even when, as sometimes happened, a Hogarthian world of social squalor peeped out from behind them. A 1921 case headlined GOT MEALS FROM ASHCANS described two "ragged, unwashed" sisters, seven and five years old, who fed themselves from garbage cans. Abandoned by their parents, they were passed around among relatives living "in crowded shant[ies]" who didn't want them: "At first the relatives put them on the floor at night and let them cry themselves to sleep. Later they put them along the wall on chairs which served as beds for more important members of the household. When sound asleep, Doris and Fanny would be lifted out and placed on the floor, to make the chair beds available for the real owners. They are undernourished and suffering from severe skin troubles due to the ashcan diet. . . ." Yet the story concluded: The "good stuff in [the sisters] is indestructible. They are still two sweet, good-tempered, bright little girls."

Some social problems remained taboo for decades. A case from 1921 stands out for its rarity, as well as for its discreet circumlocutions about illegitimacy: "Mildred, very young and inexperienced, left the city telling her family and friends that she had work in another city. Several months later she returned, explaining that it had been unsatisfactory. She now has a position which barely enables her to support herself. Leaving her parents, she goes out alone, on one excuse or another, as frequently as she can, and visits a place were she sees Shirley, a tiny, blue-eyed baby. Mildred's earnings are so small that she can only partially pay for the child's board. She is greatly worried over money, and feels her position keenly. So far she has concealed everything from her family and her friends, but she has almost made up her mind to take Shirley home with her and let people think what they will. She wants to do what is right, but the situation is extremely perplexing." Nineteen twenty-one being a different era, Mildred's case elicited a marriage proposal from a sympathetic reader.

In 1921 an illegitimate birth was a crisis. For decades thereafter, a reference to a broken promise of marriage accompanied any mention of illegitimacy in the pages of the appeal. The illegitimate children were always sent to a foster home, on the assumption that an unmarried mother was an inappropriate parent.

In its early years the Hundred Neediest Cases exerted an enormous pull on New Yorkers' imaginations, even finding its way into novels of the time. The appeal was highly individualized: contributors could earmark their donations for a specific case, and each case listed a specific amount needed—at most, several hundred dollars. Donors therefore had a sense of making an immediate difference in individual lives.

The stock market crash of 1929 passed without mention in the Neediest Cases appeal, but the Great Depression most definitely did not. The appeal's response to the depression is a telling moment in its early history. On the eve of the welfare state's birth, the fund stressed its own voluntary nature: "The fate of these hundred cases rests entirely with the conscience of the reader. There is no compulsion to give." Rather than using the depression as a lever for its fund-raising, the charity drive sharply distinguished its purpose from that of the public welfare programs just then being launched. The Neediest Cases, the *Times* said in 1933, were "victims not of economic storms but of life itself," having "been stricken with still greater misfortune [than unemployment]." The paper worried that the "ill, the helpless, the deserted ones" would be overlooked in the nation's massive response to joblessness.

And indeed, the cases from the thirties were no different from those of the preceding two decades. As ever, the paper stressed the moral qualities of the recipients. A case from 1933 crystallized the genre: "No combination of troubles, it seems, can quench the spirit of Selina G. At 71 she is sick in a hospital ward. After a lifetime of struggle, she thinks up 'last lines' to speak to the welfare visitor: 'Good-bye. I'll see you next week. That is if I don't elope.' . . . A half century ago, while she was still a young bride, Selina had to support her husband, whose lungs had become affected by his work in a tannery. She did this for the twenty years he lived, a confirmed invalid. She kept on supporting herself by domestic service until stomach ulcers forced her to stop two years ago. . . . Then she was taken to the hospital, a very sick old woman and a little frightened, though she tried to hide that with her badinage."

129

As public relief programs grew in scope, however, the fund had to confront its relationship to them. "It will be asked, quite understandably, why private charity should be necessary in these days when the government is providing relief on so vast a scale," acknowledged the *Times* in 1937. The answer to this question, posed almost yearly over the next two decades, was in constant flux. Sometimes the *Times* would explain that the fund attended to matters of the spirit while public relief tended to material needs; other times, that the fund helped those who did not qualify for public assistance; and at yet others, that the fund provided specialized services (such as rehabilitation and medicine) unavailable publicly. But no matter how the *Times* defined the fund's role vis-à-vis welfare, up through the sixties it always presented public relief as an act of remarkable generosity on the part of the public, not as an entitlement.

If the appeal's sunny disposition toward public relief appears refreshingly innocent today, that is because welfare did not represent the same constellation of problems as it does now. "We didn't worry about long-term dependency back then," recalls Arthur Gelb, a former *Times* managing editor, who wrote the Neediest Cases profiles in 1944 and 1945. Today Gelb oversees the appeal as president of the New York Times Company Foundation. The forties were a more innocent world, he says: "The stigma of going on relief was so great that it was inconceivable to stay on. People kept their heads high." Even the movies reinforced the ideal of independence, Gelb recalls: "All the heroes had an idea: get out of poverty, get a job, because you have to earn a living on your own." The appeal itself constantly lauded the work ethic.

In December 1942 the *Times*'s front page rang with news of battles between the Allies and the Axis powers in Tunisia and Burma. Locally, juvenile delinquency in New York City schools was rising, a fact attributed to the war. Opening the 1942 drive, the *Times* posed its regular question: "'Is it possible,' you may ask, 'that in these days of public relief and war employment there are still those who need my aid?'" Its answer this time—and from then on—stressed the fund's newest priorities: counseling and therapy. "Psychological problems," the paper said, "are often more pressing than physical ones." For the first time, in 1942 the *Times* included the cost of counseling in the amount requested for each case.

The rise in juvenile delinquency certainly confirmed a growing spiritual malaise. But in contrast to older models of social work, which had stressed the moral reformation of the poor, the Hundred Neediest Cases increasingly incorporated trendy psychoanalytic explanations for, and responses to, social problems. Lack of "self-fulfillment" was starting to take its place among recognized personal ills. A 1942 case was headlined BEGINNING TO FIND HERSELF; another case described an aspiring artist burdened with a guardian aunt, wholly unsympathetic to her artistic hopes, who believed that the girl's proper place was at the lingerie counter of a department store.

A few cases began to anticipate, faintly, today's pervasive social dislocations. One described a baby found bruised, with a swollen forehead. The mother, picked up roaming the streets, claimed that the child had injured herself. The unemployed father had "irresponsibly" deserted the family, said the *Times*. But both society's and the *Times*'s response to such problems remained firmly moral, rooted in notions of individual responsibility. The mother was committed to an asylum, the child put up for adoption—both actions based on recognition of the mother's unfitness. In those days the *Times* did not shrink from labeling parents irresponsible or incompetent.

The postwar years saw the triumph of the psychoanalytic model. Contemporary thinking about family relations found

131

its way into the drive, particularly the newly fashionable problem of "overly strict" child rearing, which reflected the emerging elite condemnation of traditional families. The case histories presented illegitimacy and juvenile delinquency as products of repressive childhoods, and social workers taught parents to give their straying children more freedom as an antidote to "rebellion."

Other family dramas unfolded in the Neediest Cases: a mother in 1949 was "terrified of becoming the kind of mother [her] mother was"; a periodically abandoned wife and mother was counseled to gain a "more objective view of her marriage" with an eye toward divorce. Social ties were starting to loosen—divorce was growing more prevalent, children more unmanageable. In one 1949 case a twenty-one-year-old woman, who "never felt she had a real home" because her parents had divorced, had an illegitimate son after her lover broke his marriage promise. Six years later the son had become a troublemaker and petty thief. According to the *Times*, a "psychiatric examination showed that his problems stemmed largely from a need for more attention from his mother." On the advice of the Brooklyn Bureau of Social Service, the mother quit her job and went on public assistance so as to give her son the "companionship he craves."

Such wrongheaded intervention in the lives of troubled families would go on to have a long history in the Neediest Cases. To take one example from our own day, a story in early 1996 headlined THERAPY HELPS A PROTECTIVE MOTHER COPE told an unintentionally heartbreaking tale of traditional values destroyed by liberal elites. A Guyanese single mother was allegedly causing "stress" in her son with her "rigid rules" against jeans and sneakers—rules more appropriate, the *Times* noted with alarm, for a British private school. Then the mother started having her own "stress" and discovered, through therapy, that she had repressed her memories of childhood sexual abuse—the Holy Grail of counseling. Now, presumably freed from the demons that had erupted in so cruel a dress code for her son, the mother has loosened her restrictions on him. The counseling—by an older but no wiser Brooklyn Bureau of Community Service, now renamed—succeeded: he now sports an earring and baggy pants, the *Times* reported proudly.

As if in recognition of the changing emphasis of the fund, the *Times* in 1949 stopped listing the amount needed for each case, explaining that a dollar amount could not be put on the "psychological help" that the charitable agencies now provided. The earlier notion that a reader could provide the entire amount needed to help a specific individual get through a specific crisis gave way to the idea of more generalized, permanent assistance for ongoing social ills.

The year 1949 marked one more milestone for the appeal. The *Times* cast aside its long-standing convention of distinguishing the "deserving" from the "undeserving" poor: "What a bleak world it would be if we helped only those who were thoroughly blameless! A good many of us make our own bad luck, and we suppose that some of the people represented in the Neediest Cases would not be in trouble now if they had managed their lives differently. It may even be appropriate once in a while, when help is asked, to recall Lord Chesterfield's words: 'Do not refuse your charity even to those who have no merit but their misery.' "

One can only guess why the *Times* acknowledged the self-made bad luck of some of the Neediest Cases. Most likely the changing nature of the caseload simply forced itself upon the paper's attention. While the classic pure victims—widows and orphans—still generously leavened the appeal, they were matched by more troubling cases of family disintegration and irresponsibility—relatively innocuous compared with the raging social pathologies that would show up two decades later, but nevertheless noticeably different from the uplifting stories of triumph over adversity that dominated the first appeals.

Nineteen fifty-six was a year of extraordinary prosperity at home and increasing tension abroad. Cold-war conscious- ness infused even the appeal itself. The "health of a demo- cratic society like ours" depends on voluntary assistance, wrote the city and state welfare directors in their statement on private philanthropy, a feature of the appeal since the Great Depression.

That same issue of the *Times* also contained a full-page ad for Elvis Presley's "latest and greatest" album, signaling the explosive arrival of the youth culture that peacetime prosper- ity had spawned. The 1956 Neediest Cases Fund documented the underside of that culture with an unprecedented amount of juvenile delinquency and gang activity. Children were growing disturbed and unmanageable.

By the sixties, all hell had broken loose. Truancy, delin- quency, failure at school, illegitimacy, and parental abandon- ment pervaded the cases. The first case in 1965, headlined WAITING, described two children, two and three years old, who had been deserted by their mother in front of a candy store. "My mummy said to wait here," the three-year-old explained. In another case an eleven-year-old with a shiftless, rowdy father was described as fitting the "familiar pattern of the pre- delinquent." A father was arrested for molesting a neighbor's child. Several of the cases had attempted suicide, some in their teens.

The prosperity of the 1950s reached still greater heights in the 1960s, yet suddenly everybody seemed to be talking about poverty. In 1962, Michael Harrington published *The Other America*, which set the stage for the federal War on Poverty by arguing that America had ignored millions of poor people who had been victimized by the same forces that were making most Americans prosper. New York mayor John Lindsay launched his own local war on poverty when he came into office in 1965. It included a demand, announced on the first day of the 1965 Neediest Cases appeal, for federal job-training money for women who were "family heads"—signaling the start of a fateful campaign to normalize and destigmatize the unmarried welfare-dependent mother.

In the midst of this ferment over poverty, the Neediest Cases Fund made a startling, if only implicit, acknowledgment: welfare dependency had become a problem. In their annual statement on behalf of the appeal, the state and city welfare commissioners argued that "the rehabilitation of dependent people requires the skilled help of the voluntary agency staffs, the pioneers in this field." Suddenly, the fund's purpose was no longer to assist the helpless but to wean the dependent off government aid—a monumental shift, which passed without further mention. Its implications, though, were huge: rather than eliminating poverty, the massive public effort to end it had worsened it, at least among younger, able-bodied people.

For all the social disintegration that was showing up in the appeal, one taboo remained—against the normalization of illegitimacy. As in past years, when women profiled in the appeal had an illegitimate child, the assumed next step was putting the child up for adoption. In one 1965 case, for example, a social worker was said to be helping an unwed nineteen-year-old mother "face up to the decision she must make" to relinquish her baby. But this long-standing social consensus was under attack. Already 90 percent of the 311,000 children in the city receiving public assistance were without a male parent in the household.

By 1969 the Hundred Neediest Cases Fund had hit the

135

rock bottom of social squalor. The appeal itself recognized that the era was one of "growing social disorganization." Welfare was spiraling out of control both in the city and nationwide, thanks to the welfare-rights movement. New York's rolls were rising at a monthly rate of seventeen thousand—triple what Mayor Lindsay's budget had forecast. Crime, too, was out of control; the National Commission on the Causes and Prevention of Violence called American cities a "mixture of fortresses and places of terror."

The *Times*'s fund put faces on these troubling trends. In one case a drug-addicted mother had disappeared two years previously, the father was bringing women home and locking out his two teenage children overnight, the daughter was pregnant by an older man, and the mother, recently released from jail and back in touch, wanted the son to come live with her. In another case the ten-year-old daughter of a heroin-addicted father and a paroled drug-dealer mother said she remembered strange teenagers shooting up in her kitchen. An out-of-wedlock son of a nineteen-year-old mother, who was herself illegitimate and had lived "on the streets" since she was fifteen, languished in a foster home, hostage to the mother's refusal to give him up for adoption. Truancy and delinquency were rampant, and more and more of the pro-filed teen mothers were keeping their children and going on public assistance. The underclass had taken over the fund in a big way.

As the social and moral disintegration mounted, the *Times* made a profound change in its editorial line on the Neediest Cases Fund. Gone were the holiday paeans to the generosity of ordinary citizens; gone, too, was the paper's honesty about self-induced misfortune. Instead, this was the moment that the *Times* turned sour and became an apologist for the welfare state. The editorial opening the 1969 campaign began: "The fifty-eighth annual appeal for New York's Hundred Neediest Cases arrives at a moment in this country, state and city when there is some confusion about the poor among us and what they desire. Much of this talk has been ill-informed and theoretical, taking the harsh line that penury and despair are self-induced and that financial aid is going to the lazy and undeserving." The *Times* insisted that the appeal represented people "trapped in prisons of circumstance."

This one editorial contained in miniature the agenda for the cultural elite for the next two decades: first, to deny that welfare had become a trap and that conditions in the inner city reflected a moral, as much as an economic, decline; second, to disparage as greedy, unfeeling, and possibly even racist those who questioned the welfare status quo; and third, to insist that individuals acted not of their own free will but because of environmental conditions beyond their control.

The modern era of the Neediest Cases had begun. From now on, the appeal would evolve into an increasingly strident and political platform for welfare advocacy. The moral certainties of the first decades of the appeal dissolved into a dogmatic "open-mindedness" about the various "life-style choices" that resulted in apparent need.

The format of the Hundred Neediest Cases appeal changed radically after 1972. That was the last year the *Times* printed profiles of all the cases simultaneously. It was also the last year the appeal was called the "Hundred Neediest Cases"; thereafter it became just the "Neediest Cases" and presented only one or two profiles at a time sporadically over many weeks. The *Times* never acknowledged or explained the change, but the nature of the few cases presented in 1972 may suggest a reason. Just one conveys the unprecedented degradation that now confronted *Times* readers: "Jennie" was a pregnant seventeen-year-old who had been raped by one of her mother's live-in "men friends." One brother was in jail for pushing heroin; the other two used drugs; she herself started using at age thirteen. Drugs had probably already affected her unborn child. She had attempted suicide. Catholic Charities was going to help her apply for public assistance so that "she will be free of her family and not have to depend on her friends." No mention was made of adoption: social service agencies by then embraced the view that single mothers should get public support to raise their illegitimate children.

Such social pathologies certainly were a challenge to the charitable impulse. For many years thereafter, instead of spotlighting the recipients, the appeal ran stories primarily on the agencies that distributed Neediest Cases money. One such profile, describing how the Community Service Society worked to divert youth in the South Bronx from the "delinquent-labeling process of the juvenile courts," seemed oblivious to the fact that some *Times* readers would deem the label "juvenile delinquent" perfectly appropriate for a teen criminal and wouldn't appreciate efforts to return such thugs to the streets.

A new Neediest Cases genre sprang up in the early seventies: bellyaching by the agencies about government cuts. Gone were the days of gratitude for public welfare; now the appeal regularly berated the public and the government for stinginess in supporting the poor. In 1973, as the front page followed the course of the Arab oil embargo, the appeal quoted Marina S. Heiskell, chair of the Community Service Society of New York, as saying: "We have witnessed an unbelievable trend of government cutbacks in health and welfare programs. The age-old public hostility toward the poor has not decreased, and alienation among groups—young and old, black and white, rich and poor—have [*sic*] even grown. At a time when there is more and more for us to do, we are faced with less and less to do it with."

Editorially the paper echoed the agencies' complaints: "Government funds, which were never plentiful," it moaned, "are dwindling." Just three years previously, the state and city welfare directors had noted with satisfaction government's "unprecedented" commitment, "in effort and in funds, to the alleviation of . . . mass deprivation." It was now taboo to mention that by any historical measure, welfare spending was extraordinarily high.

In 1975, the depth of New York City's financial crisis, the agencies reiterated their complaints against government budget cuts. Welfare benefits were too low, complained a director of the Community Service Society (though, of course, high welfare benefits were one cause of the city's budget crisis); the vice president of the Federation of Protestant Welfare Agencies, Joyce P. Austin, charged that the public was blind to the effect of the budget cuts. By now the appeal had become as much a mechanism for trying to boost public funding of the social service agencies as for inspiring private giving.

By 1981 the blame-the-government theme of the appeal had become explicitly political. Joyce Austin singled out President Reagan for "sweeping" and "unprecedented" cuts in food stamps, welfare, subsidized housing, and job-training services, she said, that "support the very essentials of life," as if government services, not individual initiative, support life.

During the seventies and early eighties, the *Times* generally refrained from such blame-the-government tirades. No more. The 1996 appeal opened editorially with as sensational a statement of the theme as the most radical agency directors might make: "The children, the sick, the elderly and the poor, who make up the most defenseless elements of New York City's population," the paper charged, "have suffered brutal blows from cutbacks in government services in recent years. The signs of trouble are as visible as the homeless in the streets, the abandoned buildings and the abused children in the headlines." The imagery equated welfare cutbacks with physical assault, and indeed the editorial went on to blame fatal child abuse on inadequate government welfare spending. Wholly absent was any sense of individual responsibility for creating or solving social problems.

The fund's spokesmen and recipients blame the public as well as the government for creating or contributing to poverty—despite unprecedented spending on the poor and the unprecedented openness of today's economy and society. On the fund's seventy-fifth anniversary in 1986, Thomas DiStefano, head of the Catholic Charities of Brooklyn, declared that the problems facing the poor have not changed over the years: "Many people are still burdened by poverty, discrimination, and injustice," he said—in other words, society's supposed racism and lack of justice are responsible for individual need. The then-president of the fund from the *Times*, Fred Hechinger, called "the plight of the homeless . . . a mark of public shame," his assumption being that public hard-heartedness is to blame, not advocate-driven policies that keep disturbed people from getting needed medical care.

In the new Alice-in-Wonderland world of the Neediest Cases appeal, charity heads, echoed by the *Times*, belittle the efficacy of the private charity they are soliciting. "It's naive and disingenuous for anyone to say that private charities can fill the gap [of congressional welfare cuts]," sniffed Megan E. McLaughlin, head of the Federation of Protestant Welfare Agencies, in 1995. Such talk suggests how little private charity seems to matter to these private agencies, which have come to rely more and more on government funding and to view themselves as handmaidens of the welfare state. Adolph Ochs, the founder of the Neediest Cases Fund, would have found this contempt for private initiatives astounding. Upon buying the *Times* in 1896, Ochs declared his philosophy: the paper would be devoted to sound money, low taxes, and "no more government than is absolutely necessary to protect society, maintain individual and vested rights, and assure the free exercise of a sound conscience."

Not only do the Neediest Cases charities value government welfare spending more than private donations, but much of their current charitable work, as profiled in the appeal, consists of signing up people for government assistance or fighting to restore benefits. Donors to the fund, therefore, pay twice: first, their donation is used to *obtain* welfare; then their taxes are used to *pay* welfare. A 1995 profile of the Community Service Society, for example, described a fifty-three-year-old Vietnam veteran who had lost his welfare benefits for failure to comply with the finger-imaging requirement. The veteran claimed he hadn't been informed of the requirement—a universal explanation among welfare recipients whenever they are penalized. The Community Service Society represented the veteran on appeal and won his benefits back.

And who are the victims who appear in the profiles today? Drug abuse still rages through the cases—a boyfriend on crack sets fire to the house of his companion, an unwed mother; a girl who began using drugs at age fifteen has five children by age eighteen; a grandmother cares for the abandoned children of her addicted daughter. The *Times* has even found a place for the victims of middle-class disorders. As one especially memorable profile opened, "The anorexia began during a cruise to the Bahamas."

Though the fund still profiles elderly widows, disabled breadwinners, and handicapped children, an overwhelming number of contemporary cases stem from one simple fact: having children out of wedlock. Take away illegitimacy and much of the Neediest Cases caseload would disappear. From the out-of-wedlock births in the appeal follows a predictable string of setbacks, including welfare dependency, homelessness, drug use, and often prostitution. The convention of mentioning a thwarted intention to marry has long since withered away; today many of the appeal's illegitimate births could be immaculate conceptions, for all the mention of a father.

Today's typical case is a garden-variety welfare mother. One unwed mother of four left New York for rural Florida when her relationship with her children's father broke up. She didn't like it there ("It was like Mayberry," she explains) and returned to Harlem. After a brief stint living with a son, she declared herself homeless and got a city-subsidized apartment in the Bronx, where she lives on welfare. Though it's a tight fit in the apartment, the *Times* reassures its readers, the family is managing. This saga, in the woman's view and the *Times*'s, demonstrates true grit: "It's like you have to fight to survive. That's what makes New York New York, I guess," she announces. Presumably as proof of her strong passion for justice, the *Times* notes glowingly that she lectures subway passengers for not giving money to a panhandling couple claiming AIDS.

As this case suggests, worthiness is now quite a flexible concept for the appeal. A measure of how far we have come from the virtuous widows and orphans of Adolph Ochs's time is the case of a Puerto Rican woman who, despite admitting to $10,000 of welfare fraud, now lives in a subsidized apartment on food stamps, welfare payments, and child support. Luz Pena's story epitomizes the *Times*'s current value-free approach to need. In the first half of the century, her successful bilking of the welfare system would have placed her in Ochs's category of "professional beggars"; now, however, the fund views her as needy because the deduction of restitution from her welfare check leaves just $80. Pena is emblematic of modern social welfare theory, wherein the sole criterion for assistance is material want; playing by the rules is no longer relevant.

The *Times* considers no one's opportunities so golden that the failure to take advantage of them is condemnable. Consider a 1996 profile of a seventeen-year-old with a drinking problem. The story begins with a deliberate attempt to jolt the reader: "Jennifer M. did not drink much in the mornings, maybe a swig of vodka at home or a beer on her way to school, just enough to make a teenage alcoholic feel that she could face the day." Jennifer began drinking at age fourteen, while on scholarship at a Brooklyn prep school. " 'It was more of a party thing,' she said. 'We were young. It was fun. . . . The 10th and 11th grades were a blur to me.' " Now in a rehab program, she has had several relapses—smoking marijuana with friends and nearly drinking herself into a coma at a club—but had been clean for three months at the time of the article.

Jennifer's story is indeed a sorry affair, and it is good that she is getting help. But her predicament is not a fact of nature but a product of her reprehensible behavior, made all the worse by her squandering a free prep-school education. The *Times* treats the situation as if individual will or responsibility never entered the picture. Had the paper cast the story in terms of a fall and redemption, had it acknowledged the moral challenge Jennifer faced, it would have made a more sympathetic—and certainly a more honest—case. But in the *Times*'s world, all victims look alike.

Even when modern cases seem to echo the early ones, they do so in an oddly dissonant key. The "little mother"—a young girl bereft of her mother, struggling to raise her brothers and sisters—was a mainstay of the early appeal and proved particularly moving to the *Times*'s readers. A similar situation in the 1996 appeal—a fourteen-year-old orphan named Kenya Eubanks, being raised by her twenty-one-year-

143

old sister—sounds familiar until you read on: the elder sister has a three-year-old illegitimate child; both girls are on public assistance. In an earlier age the assumption would be that such a household needs adult supervision: the older sister is already struggling with Kenya's boy problems and failure to do her homework. In today's climate the social worker got them their own apartment. In such a situation the chance that Kenya will herself reach age eighteen without having had a child seems small.

The Neediest Cases Fund still accomplishes wonderful things: it rehabilitates the disabled, sends handicapped children to camp, and buys glasses for nearly blind widows. But its unwillingness to render judgment on self-destructive behavior is part of a moral climate that has done real and lasting harm to the poor. Elite opinion contributed to the creation of today's underclass and must take some responsibility for reforming it. It is not enough to change welfare programs, to let responsibilities devolve to states and localities, to emphasize work over entitlement. We must once again start to draw moral distinctions in our public discourse—to praise virtue and blame vice. In this all-important task of cultural renewal, the *Times* continues to stand squarely in the way, stubbornly clinging to the destructive views it has done so much to disseminate.

[1997]

HEATHER MAC DONALD

The Billions of Dollars That Made Things Worse

IF THE PRACTICAL VISIONARIES who established America's great philanthropic foundations could see their legacy today, they might regret their generosity. Once an agent of social good, those powerful institutions have become a political battering ram targeted at American society. You can instantly grasp how profoundly foundations have changed by comparing two statements made by presidents of the Carnegie Corporation just a generation apart. In 1938 the corporation commissioned a landmark analysis of black-white relations from sociologist Gunnar Myrdal; the result, *An American Dilemma*, would help spark the civil rights movement. Yet Carnegie president Frederick Keppel was almost apologetic about the foundation's involvement with such a vexed social problem: "Provided the foundation limits itself to its proper function," Keppel wrote in the book's introduction, "namely, to make the facts available and then let them speak for themselves, and does not undertake to instruct the public as to what to do about them, studies of this kind provide a wholly proper and . . . sometimes a highly important use of [its] funds."

Three decades later, Carnegie president Alan Pifer's 1968 annual report reads like a voice from another planet. Abandoning Keppel's admirable restraint, Pifer exhorts his comrades in the foundation world to help shake up "sterile institutional forms and procedures left over from the past" by supporting "aggressive new community organizations which . . . the comfortable stratum of American life would consider disturbing and perhaps even dangerous." No longer content to provide mainstream knowledge dispassionately, America's most prestigious philanthropies now aspired to revolutionize what they believed to be a deeply flawed American society.

The results, from the 1960s onward, have been devastating. Foundation-supported poverty advocates fought to make welfare a right—and generations have grown up fatherless and dependent. Foundation-funded minority advocates fought for racial separatism and a vast system of quotas—and American society remains perpetually riven by the issue of race. On most campuses today, a foundation-endowed multicultural circus has driven out the very idea of a common culture, deriding it as a relic of American imperialism. Foundation-backed advocates for various "victim" groups use the courts to bend government policy to their will, thwarting the democratic process. And poor communities across the country often find their traditional values undermined by foundation-sent "community activists" bearing the latest fashions in diversity and "enlightened" sexuality. The net effect is not a more just but a more divided and contentious American society.

Not all foundations adopted the cause of social change, of course; but the overwhelmingly "progressive" large foundations set the tone for the entire sector—especially such giants as Ford, which got radicalized in the sixties, and Rockefeller and Carnegie, which followed suit in the seventies. Such foundations wield enormous financial might: a mere 2 percent of all foundations (or 1,020) provide more than half of the approximately $10 billion that foundations now give away each year, and in 1992 the 50 largest foundations accounted for more than one-quarter of all foundation spending. Though some conservative foundations have recently risen to prominence, Smith College sociologist Stanley Rothman has found that liberal foundations still outnumber conservative ones three to one, and that liberal policy groups receive four times as much foundation money and four times as many grants as their conservative counterparts. The Ford Foundation gave $42 million in grants to education and culture alone in 1994, while the Olin Foundation, the premier funder of conservative scholarship on campus, spent only $13 million on all its programs, educational and non-educational. Understanding the impact of foundations on American culture so far, therefore, means concentrating on the liberal leviathans.

In their early, heroic period, foundations provided a luminous example of how private philanthropy can improve the lives of millions around the world. Key institutions of modern American life—the research university, the professional medical school, the public library—owe their existence to the great foundations, which had been created in the modern belief that philanthropy should address the causes rather than the effects of poverty.

There was no more articulate exponent of the new philanthropic philosophy than Andrew Carnegie, a self-educated Scot who rose from impoverished bobbin boy in a textile mill to head America's largest coal and steel complex. He elaborated his theory of "scientific philanthropy," a capitalist's response to Marx's "scientific socialism," in *The Gospel of Wealth* (1889), an eloquent testament and a stinging rebuke to many a contemporary foundation executive.

The growing abyss between the vast industrial fortunes and the income of the common laborer, Carnegie argued, was the inevitable result of the most beneficial economic system that mankind had ever known. The tycoon, however, merely held his fortune in trust for the advancement of the common good; moreover, he should give away his wealth during his lifetime, using the same acumen that he showed in making it. The scientific philanthropist will target his giving to "help those who will help themselves," creating institutions through which those working poor with a "divine spark" can better themselves economically and spiritually. The "slothful, the drunken, [and] the unworthy" were outside his scheme: "One man or woman who succeeds in living comfortably by begging is more dangerous to society, and a greater obstacle to the progress of humanity, than a score of wordy Socialists," he pronounced.

Starting in 1901, Carnegie threw himself full-time into practicing what he preached. He created one of the greatest American institutions for social mobility: the free public library, which he built and stocked in nearly two thousand communities. He established the Carnegie Institute of Technology (now the Carnegie Mellon University); the Carnegie Foundation for the Advancement of Teaching, to provide pensions for all college teachers; a museum; a scientific research institute; a university trust; Carnegie Hall in New York City; the World Court building in the Hague; and a host of other major institutions. A Carnegie-commissioned report on medical education revolutionized medical training, sparking reforms that would give the U.S. the greatest medical schools in the world. Even so, his wealth grew faster than he could give it away. Finally "in desperation," according to his biographer, he created the Carnegie Corporation in 1911.

During the early years of this century, the press kept tabs on a remarkable philanthropic rivalry: would Andrew Carnegie or John D. Rockefeller give away the most money? Rockefeller created overnight the great University of Chicago from a third-rate Baptist college in 1892. He established the renowned Rockefeller Institute for Medical Research and supported the education of southern blacks. But he, too, could not make donations fast enough. So in 1909 he endowed a foundation that, in conjunction with the Rockefeller Institute, made medical history—eradicating hookworm here and abroad, establishing the first major schools of public health, developing the yellow fever vaccine, controlling a new strain of malaria, and reducing infant typhus epidemics. In later years the Rockefeller Foundation contributed to discoveries in genetics, biophysics, biochemistry, and in medical technologies like spectroscopy, X rays, and the use of tracer elements.

But the "scientific philanthropy" articulated by Rockefeller's personal advisor, Frederick Gates, contained a crucial—and ultimately destructive—innovation. The value of a foundation, Gates argued, was that it moved the disposition of wealth from the control of the donor into the hands of "experts"—precisely the opposite of Carnegie's view that the person who made the money would be its wisest administrator. Eventually, this transfer of control yielded the paradox of funds made by laissez-faire capitalists being used for the advocacy of a welfare state. Even during Rockefeller's lifetime, Gates's doctrine produced some odd moments. In 1919 Rockefeller prophetically wrote to his lawyer: "I could wish that the education which some professors furnish was more conducive to the most sane and practical and possible views of life rather than drifting . . . toward socialism and some forms of Bolshevism." But Rockefeller's attorney countered that donors should not try to influence teaching—or even consider a university's philosophy in funding it. The subsequent history of academia has proved the folly of that injunction, which Rockefeller unfortunately obeyed.

When the Ford Foundation flowered into an activist, "socially conscious" philanthropy in the 1960s, it sparked the key revolution in the foundation worldview: the idea that foundations were to improve the lot of mankind not by building lasting institutions but by challenging existing ones. Henry Ford and his son Edsel had originally created the foundation in 1936 not out of any grand philanthropic vision but instead to shelter their company's stock from taxes and to ensure continued family control of the business. When the foundation came into its full inheritance of Ford stock, it became overnight America's largest foundation by several magnitudes. Its expenditures in 1954 were four times higher than second-ranked Rockefeller and ten times higher than third-ranked Carnegie.

From its start, Ford aimed to be different, eschewing medical research and public health in favor of social issues such as First Amendment restrictions and undemocratic concentrations of power, economic problems, world peace, and social science. Nevertheless, Andrew Carnegie himself might have applauded some of Ford's early efforts, including the "Green Revolution" in high-yielding crops and its pioneering program to establish theaters, orchestras, and dance and opera companies across the country. But by the early 1960s, the trustees started clamoring for a more radical vision; according to Richard Magat, a Ford employee, they demanded "action-oriented rather than research-oriented" programs that would "test the outer edges of advocacy and citizen participation."

The first such "action-oriented" program, the Gray Areas project, was a turning point in foundation history and—because it was a prime mover of the ill-starred War on Poverty—a turning point in American history as well. Its creator, Paul Ylvisaker, an energetic social theorist from Harvard and subsequent icon for the liberal foundation community, had concluded that the problems of newly migrated urban blacks and Puerto Ricans could not be solved by the "old and fixed ways of doing things." Because existing private and public institutions were unresponsive, he argued, the new poverty populations needed a totally new institution—the "community action agency"—to coordinate legal, health, and welfare services and to give voice to the poor. According to Senator Daniel Patrick Moynihan, an early poverty warrior under Presidents Kennedy and Johnson, Ford "proposed nothing less than institutional change in the operation and control of American cities. . . . [Ford] invented a new level of American government: the inner-city community action agency." Ylvisaker proceeded to establish such agencies in Boston, New Haven, Philadelphia, and Oakland.

Most significantly, Gray Areas' ultimate purpose was to spur a similar federal effort. Ford was the first—but far from the last—foundation to conceive of itself explicitly as a laboratory for the federal welfare state. As Ylvisaker later explained, foundations should point out "programs and policies, such as social security, income maintenance, and educational entitlement that convert isolated and discretionary acts of private charity into regularized public remedies that flow as a matter of legislated right." In this vein, the foundation measured the success of Gray Areas by the number of federal visitors to the program's sites, and it declared the passage of the Economic Opportunity Act of 1964, which opened the War on Poverty and incorporated the Ford-invented community action agencies, to be Gray Areas' "proudest achievement."

Unfortunately, because it was so intent on persuading the federal government to adopt the program, Ford ignored reports that the community action agencies were failures, according to historian Alice O'Connor. Reincarnated as federal Community Action Programs (CAPs), Ford's urban cadres soon began tearing up cities. Militancy became the mark of merit for federal funders, according to Senator Moynihan. In Newark, the director of the local CAP urged blacks to arm themselves before the 1967 riots; leaflets calling for a demonstration were run off on the CAP's mimeograph machine. The federal government funneled community action money to Chicago gangs—posing as neighborhood organizers—who then continued to terrorize their neighbors. The Syracuse, New York, CAP published a remedial reading manual that declared: "No ends are accomplished without the use of force. . . . Squeamishness about force is the mark not of idealistic, but moonstruck morals." Syracuse CAP employees applied $7 million of their $8 million federal grant to their own salaries.

Ford created another of the War on Poverty's most flamboyant failures—Mobilization for Youth, a federally funded juvenile delinquency agency on Manhattan's Lower East Side that quickly expanded its sights from providing opportunity to minority youth to bringing down the "power structure." Home base for the welfare-rights movement, the Mobilization for Youth aimed to put so many people on welfare that the state and city's finances would collapse. Its techniques included dumping dead rats on Mayor Robert Wagner's doorstep and organizing Puerto Rican welfare mothers for "conflict confrontations" with local teachers.

These programs were just warm-ups, however. When McGeorge Bundy, former White House national security advisor, became Ford's president in 1966, the foundation's activism switched into high gear. Bundy reallocated Ford's resources from education to minority rights, which in 1960 had accounted for 2.5 percent of Ford's giving but by 1970 would soar to 40 percent. Under Bundy's leadership, Ford created a host of new advocacy groups, such as the Mexican-American Legal Defense and Educational Fund (a prime mover behind bilingual education) and the Native American Rights Fund, that still wreak havoc on public policy today. Ford's support for a radical Hispanic youth group in San Antonio led even liberal congressman Henry B. Gonzales to charge that Ford had fostered the "emergence of reverse racism in Texas."

Incredibly, foundation officers believed that Ford's radicalization merely responded to the popular will. As Francis X. Sutton, a longtime Ford staffer, reminisced in 1989: "It took the critical populist upsurge at the end of the sixties to weaken faith that the foundation's prime vocation lay in helping government, great universities, and research centers. . . . As the sixties wore on, the values of the New Left spread through American society and an activistic spirit entered the foundation that pulled it away from its original vision of solving the world's problems through scientific knowledge." The notion that the 1960s represented a "populist upsurge," or that New Left values bubbled up from the American grassroots rather than being actively disseminated by precisely such rich, elite institutions as the Ford Foundation, could only be a product of foundation thinking.

The most notorious Bundy endeavor, the school decentralization experiment in the Ocean Hill–Brownsville section of Brooklyn, changed the course of liberalism by fracturing the black-Jewish civil rights coalition and souring race relations in New York for years afterward. Bundy had led a may-oral panel under John Lindsay that recommended giving "community control" over local public school districts to parents. The panel's report, written by a Ford staffer, claimed that New York's huge centralized school system was not sufficiently accountable to minority populations. Black and Puerto Rican children could not learn or even behave, the report maintained, unless their parents were granted "meaningful participation" in their education. Translation: parents should hire and fire local teachers and school administrators.

Ford set about turning this theory into reality with utmost clumsiness. It chose as the head of its $1.4 million decentralization experiment in three Brooklyn school districts a long-time white-hater, Rhody McCoy, who dreamed of creating an all-black school system, right up through college, within the public schools. McCoy was a moderate, however, compared with the people he tapped as deputies. Although the school board blocked his appointment of a militant under indictment for conspiracy to murder, he did manage to hire Les Campbell, the radical head of the Afro-American Teachers Association, who organized his school's most violent students into an anti-Semitic combat force. According to education scholar Diane Ravitch, McCoy had an understanding with racist thug Sonny Carson that Carson's "bodyguards" would intimidate white teachers until McCoy would diplomatically call them off.

Ford's experimental school districts soon exploded with anti-Semitic black rage, as militants argued that black and Puerto Rican children failed because Jewish teachers were waging "mental genocide" on them. The day after Martin Luther King's assassination, students at a junior high school rampaged through the halls beating up white teachers, having been urged by Les Campbell to "[s]end [whitey] to the grave-yard" if he "taps you on the shoulder."

154

When the teachers' union struck to protest the illegal firing of nineteen teachers deemed "hostile" to decentralization, parent groups, mostly Ford-funded, responded with hostile boycotts. McCoy refused to reinstate the nineteen teachers, though ordered by the school board to do so. White teachers at one school found an anti-Semitic screed in their mailboxes, calling Jews "Blood-sucking Exploiters and Murderers" and alleging that "the So-Called Liberal Jewish Friend . . . is Really Our Enemy and He is Responsible For the Serious Educational Retardation of Our Black Children." McCoy refused to denounce the pamphlet or the anti-Semitism behind it. Nor did Ford publicly denounce such tactics—or take responsibility after the fact. McGeorge Bundy later sniffed self-righteously: "If private foundations cannot assist experiments, their unique role will be impaired, to the detriment of American society." But if the experiment goes awry, the foundation can saunter off, leaving the community to pick up the pieces.

Dean Rusk, president of the Rockefeller Foundation in the late 1950s, once described Ford's influence on other foundations: What the "fat boy in the canoe does," he said, "makes a difference to everybody else." And Ford's influence was never stronger than after it adopted the cause of social change. Waldemar Nielsen's monumental studies of foundations, published in 1972 and 1985, only strengthened the Ford effect, for Nielsen celebrated activist philanthropy and berated those foundations that had not yet converted to the cause. "As a result," recalls Richard Larry, president of the Sarah Scaife Foundation, "a number of foundations said: 'If this is what the foundation world is doing and what the experts say is important, we should move in that direction, too.'" The Rockefeller Brothers Fund, for example, funded the National Welfare Rights Organization—at the same time that the organization was demonstrating against Governor Nelson Rockefeller of New York. The Carnegie Corporation pumped nearly $20

155

million into various left-wing advocacy groups during the 1970s.

Many foundations had turned against the system that had made them possible, as Henry Ford II recognized when he quit the Ford Foundation board in disgust in 1977. "In effect," he wrote in his resignation letter, "the foundation is a creature of capitalism, a statement that, I'm sure, would be shocking to many professional staff people in the field of philanthropy. It is hard to discern recognition of this fact in anything the foundation does. It is even more difficult to find an understanding of this in many of the institutions, particularly the universities, that are the beneficiaries of the foundation's grant programs."

Did Ford exaggerate? Not according to Robert Schrank, a Ford program officer during the 1970s and early 1980s. Schrank, a former Communist, recalls the "secret anti-capitalist orientation" of his fellow program officers. "People were influenced by the horror stories we Marxists had put out about the capitalist system," he says; "it became their guidance."

Naturally, Henry Ford's resignation had no effect; the doctrine of independence from the donor had taken full root. As McGeorge Bundy coolly remarked: "He has a right to expect people to read his letter carefully, but I don't think one letter from anyone is going to change the foundation's course."

Today, the full-blown liberal foundation worldview looks like this: First, white racism is the cause of black and Hispanic social problems. In 1982, for example, Carnegie's Alan Pifer absurdly accused the country of tolerating a return to "legalized segregation of the races." The same note still sounds in Rockefeller president Peter C. Goldmark Jr.'s assertion, in his 1995 annual report, that we "urgently need . . . a national conversation about race . . . to talk with candor about the implications of personal and institutional racism."

Second, Americans discriminate widely on the basis not just of race but also of gender, "sexual orientation," class, and ethnicity. As a consequence, victim groups need financial support to fight the petty-mindedness of the majority.

Third, Americans are a selfish lot. Without the creation of court-enforced entitlement, the poor will be abused and ignored. Without continuous litigation, government will be unresponsive to social needs.

Fourth, only government can effectively ameliorate social problems. Should government cut welfare spending, disaster will follow, which no amount of philanthropy can cure.

And finally, as a corollary to tenet four: at heart, most social problems are economic ones. In the language of foundations, America has "disinvested" in the poor. Only if the welfare state is expanded into "new areas of need," to quote Pifer, will the poor be able to succeed. This worldview is particularly noticeable in three key areas of foundation funding: the dissemination of diversity ideology, the "collaboratives" movement in community development, and public interest litigation and advocacy.

A worry for the liberal foundations in the 1970s, "diversity" became an all-consuming obsession in the 1980s. Foundation boards and staffs got "diversified," sometimes producing friction and poor performance. "Foundations were so anxious to show that they, too, had their black and Puerto Rican that hiring decisions entailed mediocrity," says Gerald Freund, a former program officer with the Rockefeller and MacArthur foundations. Some foundations, led by Ford, started requiring all grant applicants to itemize the racial and gender composition of their staff and trustees, sometimes to their great bewilderment. One organization dedicated to Eastern Europe was told that its funder expected more minorities on its board. No problem, replied a charmingly naive European ambassador; how about a Kurd or Basque trustee? He soon learned that that is not what funders mean by "minorities." Organizations that already represent a minority interest—an Asian organization, say—might be told to find an American Indian or a Hispanic board member. "It is stunning to me," laments the executive director of one of Washington's most liberal policy groups, "that it is no longer crucially important whether my organization is succeeding; the critical issue is the color complexion of my staff."

Universities have proved unswervingly devoted soldiers in the foundations' diversity crusade. It was in the sixties that Ford put its money behind black studies, setting up a model for academic ghettoization that would be repeated endlessly over the next thirty years. Today, many universities recall the Jim Crow South, with separate dorms, graduation ceremonies, and freshman initiation programs for different ethnic groups, in a gross perversion of the liberal tradition. Students in foundation-funded ethnic studies courses learn that Western culture (whose transmission is any university's principal reason for existence) is the source of untold evil rather than of the "rights" they so vociferously claim.

Lavishly fertilized with foundation money, women's studies—those campus gripe sessions peppered with testimonials to one's humiliation at the hands of the "patriarchy"—debased the curriculum further into divisive victimology. From 1972 to 1992, women's studies received $36 million from Ford, Rockefeller, Carnegie, Mott, and Mellon, among others. Foundation-funded research centers on women, such as the Center for Research on Women at Wellesley College, established with Carnegie money, sprang up on campuses nationwide. The Wellesley Center's most visible accomplishment is the wildly influential—and wholly spurious—report "How Schools Shortchange Girls," which claims that secondary education subjects girls to incessant gender bias. Not to be outshone, Ford produced a multilingual translation of the report for distribution at the Beijing global women's conference. Rockefeller, taking diversity several steps further, funds humanities fellowships at the University of Georgia for "womanists"—defined as "black feminists or feminists of color"—and supports the City University of New York's Center for Lesbian and Gay Studies.

Not content with setting up separate departments of ethnic and gender studies, foundations have poured money into a powerful movement called "curriculum transformation," which seeks to inject race, gender, and sexual consciousness into *every* department and discipline. A class in biology, for example, might consider feminine ways of analyzing cellular metabolism; a course in music history might study the hidden misogyny in Beethoven's Ninth Symphony—actual examples. One accomplishment of the curricular transformationists is to distinguish bad, "masculine" forms of thinking (logic, mathematics, scientific research) from good, "feminine" forms, which subordinate the search for right answers to "inclusiveness" and "wholeness." At the University of Massachusetts, Boston, the recipient of a Ford curriculum transformation grant, a course is not culturally diverse if it addresses "gender" one week and "social class" the next, according to the university's diversity coordinator. "We'd want the issues of diversity addressed every week," she says. Edgar Beckham, a program officer in charge of Ford's Campus Diversity Initiative, lets his imagination run wild in describing the enormous reach of diversity: "Every domain of institutional activity might be involved," he says—"buildings, grounds, financial aid." No domain, in other words, is safe from foundation intervention.

The big foundations pursue identity politics and multiculturalism just as obsessively in the performing and fine arts. Gone are the days when Ford's W. McNeil Lowry, described by Lincoln Kirstein as "the single most influential patron of the performing arts the American democratic system has ever produced," collaborated with such artists as Isaac Stern to find new talent. The large foundations now practice what Robert Brustein, director of the American Repertory Theater, calls "coercive philanthropy," forcing arts institutions to conform to the foundations' vision of a multicultural paradise—one that, above all else, builds minority self-esteem.

Foundations talk a good game of inclusion, but when it comes to artistic grant-making, their outlook is color-coded. I asked Robert Curvin, vice president for communications at Ford, what would be so wrong about giving a black child the tools to appreciate, say, a Schubert song. He replied that "all art and expression begins with one's own culture. Traditionally," he added, "we did not recognize the tremendous value in conga drums. Now, we can't easily make these judgments [among different artistic forms]." Maybe not. But the view that black children are inherently suited for conga drums seems patronizing and false. Aren't American blacks as much the rightful heirs of the Western artistic tradition as other Americans?

Alison Bernstein, director of Ford's education and culture division, crystallized the liberal foundation perspective at the end of my interview with her. She had recently attended the New York City Ballet, where the audience, she noted, was "all white." Yet the success among blacks of *Bring In 'da Noise, Bring In 'da Funk*, the Tony-winning rap and tap tour through the history of black oppression, she said, shows that the "minority audience is out there." Why, she asked, isn't the New York City Ballet commissioning a work from Savion Glover, the tap prodigy behind *Bring In 'da Noise*? In other words, we can only expect blacks to come to the ballet for "black" choreography. In W. McNeil Lowry's time, her question would have been: how can we help minority students enjoy classical ballet, which will enrich them as human beings?

The second focus of the foundations' liberal zeal, the so-called "collaboratives" movement in community development, is emblematic of the thirty-year-long foundation assault on the bourgeois virtues that once kept communities and families intact. The idea behind this movement, which grows out of the failed community action programs of the 1960s, is that a group of "community stakeholders," assembled and funded by a foundation, becomes a "collaborative" to develop and implement a plan for community revitalization. That plan should be "comprehensive" and should "integrate" separate government services, favorite foundation mantras. To the extent this means anything, it sounds innocuous enough, and sometimes is. But as with the foundations' choice of community groups in the 1960s, the rhetoric of "community" and local empowerment is often profoundly hypocritical.

The Annie E. Casey Foundation's teen pregnancy initiative called Plain Talk is a particularly clear—and painful—example of the moral imperialism with which foundations impose their "progressive" values on hapless communities. In its early years, the foundation, the product of the United Parcel Service fortune, ran its own foster care and adoption agency. But when its endowment ballooned in the 1980s, the foundation jumped into the already crowded field of "social change."

Plain Talk set out to reduce unwanted teen pregnancies

not by promoting abstinence but by "encouraging local adults to engage youth in frank and open discussions regarding sexuality," in the words of the project's evaluation report, and by improving teens' access to birth control. In Casey's view, the real cause of teen pregnancies is that "adults"—note, not "parents"—haven't fully acknowledged adolescent sex or accepted teens' need for condoms. The only problem was that the values of Plain Talk were deeply abhorrent to several of the communities (often immigrant) that Casey targeted. Incredibly, Casey regarded this divergence as a "barrier" to, rather than a source of, diversity. The evaluation report, prepared by Public/Private Ventures, a youth advocacy organization, refers with obvious disgust to the "deep-rooted preference for abstinence and the desire to sugarcoat the Plain Talk message that resurfaced repeatedly. . . . Stated simply," the report sighs, "the less assimilated, more traditional Latino and Southeast Asian cultures regard premarital sex among teenagers as unacceptable. They tend to deny that it occurs in their community and do not feel it is appropriate to discuss sex openly with their children." Foundation-approved diversity is only skin-deep: Asians and Hispanics qualify only if they toe the ideological line.

Project leaders were determined to stamp out all public expressions of dissent. When members of one collaborative were heard making "judgmental" statements about teen sexuality—in other words, that teens should not have sex—Casey recommended a "values-clarification workshop" with the Orwellian goal of teaching members how to "respect their differences." Likewise, when a young male member of the San Diego collaborative brought a homemade banner for a local parade that read "Plain Talk: Say No to Sex," the project manager promptly initiated a two-hour "team discussion" that eventually pressured the boy to accept a new banner: "Plain Talk: Say No to AIDS." Chastity isn't part of the agenda.

In the struggle between a massive colonizing force and small communities valiantly trying to hold on to their beliefs, there was never any question which side would triumph. Casey had millions of dollars; the communities just had their convictions. The evaluation states unapologetically that the "struggle" to force residents to accept Plain Talk goals was "long and sometimes painful." But eventually, says the report, people came to "recognize that while their personal beliefs are valid and acceptable, they must be put aside for the sake of protecting youth."

Plain Talk's moral imperialism might be easier to swallow were there any evidence that increasing condom availability and legitimating teen sex reduced teen pregnancy. But as such evidence does not exist, Casey's condescension toward immigrants' "deeply-rooted ways of thinking" about teen sexuality, ways that for centuries kept illegitimacy at low levels, leaves a particularly bad taste.

For all its self-congratulation for having involved residents in planning "social change . . . appropriate to the conditions in their particular communities," as the evaluation puts it, Plain Talk gives the lie to the central myth of all such community initiatives: that they represent a grassroots movement. The San Diego collaborative was led by a woman the evaluation report calls an "experienced sexuality educator with a special interest in AIDS awareness and prevention, . . . respected within the influential circle of community activists and agency representatives." The foundation couldn't have come up with an occupation more repugnant to the local churchgoing Latino residents. But the "community leaders" favored by foundations do not represent the community; they represent the activists.

Yet for all its bold embrace of teen sexuality, Plain Talk was curiously unable to act on its own premises. At a Plain Talk retreat in Atlanta, rumors flew of a "sexual encounter" among teens who apparently had absorbed the Plain Talk message far too well. But rather than asking non-judgmentally, "Did you use condoms?" or offering to provide condoms for the next orgy, the adults tried to squelch the rumors, realizing they would be fatal for the reputation of the initiative. They also attempted to establish a curfew for the next retreat, igniting weeks of battle from the teens. Adolescent "empowerment," once out of the bottle, is hard to put back in.

The collaborative movement suffers from another shortcoming: a foundation planning a collaborative doesn't have the slightest idea what exactly the collaborative is supposed to do or what its source of authority will be. Take Casey's inaugural project in social change, called New Futures. The astounding theory behind the initiative, echoing Ford's Gray Areas program, was that the greatest problem facing inner-city children is the discrete nature of government services such as education and health care. Not until all social programs are integrated can we expect children to stay in school, learn, and not have babies, reasoned the foundation. Accordingly, Casey gave five cities an average of $10 million each over five years to form a collaborative consisting of leaders from business, social service agencies, schools, and the community to lead the way toward "comprehensive," integrated services for junior high students.

No one, not even the foundation officers who cooked up the idea, knew what such services would look like. Casey's mysterious pronouncements, such as a suggestion to "integrat[e] pregnancy prevention, education, and employment strategies," left the local groups as befuddled as before. The "area of greatest difficulty," concludes the New Futures evaluation report in particularly opaque foundationese, "appeared to be translating crossagency discourse into tangible operational reform that would improve the status of youth"—in other words, the project was meaningless. A Ford project for comprehensive collaborative development ran into the same difficulty of making sense of its mission. "The notion of 'integrated, comprehensive development' is a conceptual construct not easily translated into active terms," states the first-year evaluation poignantly. "Participants have struggled with what, exactly, is meant by the term." If foundation officers thought in concrete realities, not in slogans, they'd have no trouble recognizing the silliness of the idea that "categorical services" are holding children back, when for centuries schools have concentrated solely on education, hospitals solely on health care, and employers solely on business, without untoward results for the young.

Little wonder that New Futures made things worse, not better. The project's "case managers," who were supposed to coordinate existing services for individual children, yanked their young "clients" out of class for a twenty-minute chat every week or so, sending the clear message that the classroom was not important. Students in the program ended up with lower reading and writing scores, higher dropout and pregnancy rates, and no better employment or college prospects than their peers.

The third significant area of funding, public interest litigation and advocacy, embodies the foundations' long-standing goal of producing "social change" by controlling government policy. Foundations bankroll public interest law groups that seek to establish in court rights that democratically elected legislatures have rejected. Foundations thus help sustain judicial activism by supporting one side of the symbiotic relationship between activist judges and social-change-seeking lawyers.

Foundations have used litigation to create and expand the iron trap of bilingual education; they have funded the perversion of the Voting Rights Act into a costly instrument of apartheid; and they lie behind the transformation of due-process rights into an impediment to, rather than a guarantor of, justice. Foundation support for such socially disruptive litigation makes a mockery of the statutory prohibition on lobbying, since foundations can effect policy changes in the courts, under the officially approved banner of "public interest litigation," that are every bit as dramatic as those that could be achieved in the legislature.

These days, however, foundation-supported lawyers defend the status quo as often as they seek to change it; after all, foundations helped create that status quo. Foundation money is beating back efforts to reform welfare, through such Washington-based think tanks as the Center for Law and Social Policy and the Center on Budget and Policy Priorities, whose director won a MacArthur "genius" award in 1996. The Ford Foundation, the Public Welfare Foundation, the Norman Foundation, and others support the Center for Social Welfare Policy and Law in New York City, a law firm that represented the National Welfare Rights Organization during the 1960s and 1970s, when that organization was conducting its phenomenally successful campaign to legitimate welfare and encourage its spread. Today, the center is using Ford money to sue New York City over its long overdue welfare anti-fraud program. The suit apocalyptically accuses the city of depriving needy people of the "sole means available to them to obtain food, clothing, housing and medical assistance," as if welfare were the world's only conceivable means of support.

Liberal foundations are straining to block popular efforts to change the country's discriminatory racial quota system. The Rockefeller Foundation and scores of other like-minded foundations are pumping millions into the National Affirmative Action Consortium, a potpourri of left-wing advocacy groups including the NAACP Legal Defense and Educational

Fund, the Mexican-American Legal Defense and Educational Fund, the National Women's Law Center, and the Women's Legal Defense Fund. The consortium will undertake a "public education campaign" to defeat the California Civil Rights Initiative, the groundbreaking ballot measure that would allow ordinary people for the first time in history to vote on affirmative action. If passed, the measure would return California to the color-blind status intended by the federal Civil Rights Act of 1964.

The Edna McConnell Clark Foundation is among the staunchest foundation supporters of litigation and advocacy. David Hall McConnell, Edna's father, was a traveling book salesman who enticed customers with a free bottle of homemade perfume. When the perfume proved more popular than the books, the entrepreneurial McConnell started a perfume company in 1886 that became the world's largest cosmetic manufacturer, Avon. For its first twenty years, the Edna McConnell Clark Foundation supported such institutions as Lincoln Center, Smith College and Cornell University (to which it donated science buildings), the Columbia-Presbyterian Hospital, and the Woods Hole Oceanographic Institute. But in the 1970s the foundation, herded by its new professional managers, joined the stampede into activism.

No other foundation has had as dramatic an impact in shaping the debate over crime and punishment. Says Frank Hartman, executive director of the Kennedy School of Government: "I don't know what the conversation would be like in [Clark's] absence." The foundation has bankrolled the wave of prisoners' rights suits that have clogged the courts. But more important, Clark has tirelessly sponsored the specious notion that the U.S. incarcerates too many harmless criminals. In 1991 the Clark-supported Sentencing Project published a comparative study criticizing high U.S. incarceration rates,

167

which sociologist Charles Logan likens to an "undergraduate term paper—one that was badly done." Nevertheless, the study was on page one of newspapers across the country, fueling editorials and congressional speeches about America's misguided prison policies. As Logan remarks, "Foundations are propaganda machines; that is the basis of their success."

The foundation also promotes the theme that American justice is profoundly racist. It supports the Equal Justice Institute in Alabama, which sues on behalf of prisoners claiming victimization by race. The Clark-funded Sentencing Project promotes the proposed federal Racial Justice Act, which would impose racial ceilings on sentencing. By injecting race into the debate over crime, McConnell Clark is doing a great public disservice. In an era of jury nullification on the basis of racial sympathy, white racism hardly seems the criminal justice system's major problem. Moreover, the first thing you will hear in any inner-city neighborhood is "Get the dealers off the streets," not "The penalties for dealing crack are discriminatory."

The McConnell Clark Foundation has one spectacular success to show for its effort to change government policies: it has helped make New York City's homeless policies the most irrational in the nation. The foundation has been the most generous funder of the Legal Aid Society's Homeless Family Rights Project, which has been suing the city for over a decade to require immediate housing of families claiming homelessness in a private apartment with cooking facilities. Should the city fail to place every family that shows up at its doorstep within twenty-four hours (a requirement without parallel in any other city in the U.S.), Legal Aid sues for contempt, penalties, and—of course—legal fees, on top of the $200,000 McConnell Clark gives it each year.

The Clark-bankrolled project has found an eager partner

in the presiding judge, Helen Freedman, who has hit the city with over $6 million in fines. She has ordered the city to pay every allegedly homeless family that has to stay more than twenty-four hours in a city intake office between $150 and $250 a night—an extraordinary windfall. James Capoziello, former deputy general counsel in the city's Human Resources Administration, calls the litigation "one of the most asinine instances of judicial misconduct and misuses of the judiciary" he has ever seen. Says one homeless provider in the city: "It is a crime to spend scarce resources for having to sleep on the floor. With $1 million in fines you could run a fifty-unit facility for a year."

There is considerable irony to Clark's support for homelessness litigation, since it helped create the problem. According to Waldemar Nielsen, Clark funded one of the lawsuits that led to the deinstitutionalization of the mentally ill, a primary cause of homelessness today. Moreover, Clark bankrolls an array of advocacy groups responsible in large part for New York's tight housing market—groups like New York State Tenant and Neighborhood Information Services, the most powerful advocate for rent regulation in the state. Thanks to such groups, New York is the only city in the country to have maintained rent control continuously since the end of World War II, leading to one of the lowest rates of new housing construction and highest rates of abandonment in the nation.

McConnell Clark also supports organizations that campaign against the city's effort to sell its huge portfolio of tax-defaulted housing, which it operates at an enormous loss. Jay Small, director of one such organization, the Association of Neighborhood Housing Developers, believes that once the city takes title to housing, the property should never revert to private ownership but should become "socially owned." Years after the Soviet collapse, the notion that the city should become a bastion of socialized housing is hardly forward-looking.

For some of the groups McConnell Clark supports, housing is just the opening wedge to a broader transformation of society. "Ultimately, the solution to the housing crisis is to change property relations," argues Small. He explains that he is using "a code word for socialism." Rima McCoy, co-director of the Clark-funded Action for Community Empowerment, also takes an expansive view of social relations. She was asked in 1995 whether housing was a right. The question astounded her: "That anyone could even ask that kind of question—do people have an inalienable right to housing?—is just a product of our current climate," she replied, "which would have the middle class believe that the poor are the source of the current problems in the U.S."

Of course, even within the large liberal foundations, even within so seemingly monolithic a place as the Ford Foundation, there have always been pockets of sanity, where a commonsense approach to helping people and promoting stable communities has reigned. And there are some signs of more recent countercurrents to the prevailing "progressive" ethic—the Ford and Casey Foundations, for example, both trumpet their fatherhood initiatives. Yet the impulse toward the activism that over the past thirty years has led the great liberal foundations to do much more harm than good remains overwhelming. In a pathetic statement of aimlessness, the president of a once great foundation recently called up a former Ford poverty fighter to ask plaintively where all the social movements had gone.

The mega-foundations should repress their yearning for activism once and for all. The glories of early twentieth-century philanthropy were produced by working within accepted notions of social improvement, not against them.

Building libraries was not a radical act; it envisioned no transformation of property relations or redistribution of power. Andrew Carnegie merely sought to make available to a wider audience the same values and intellectual resources that had allowed him to succeed. Yes, the world has changed since Carnegie's time, but the recipe for successful philanthropy has not.

[1996]

HEATHER MAC DONALD

What Good Is Pro Bono?

FOR MOST of its history, the organized bar in America has
been conservatism incarnate, standing foursquare for the
sanctity of property rights and the rule of law. Today, there is
hardly a cause too left-wing to receive its patronage. Do you
advocate expanding entitlements, blocking welfare reform,
multiplying the victim classes, or promoting homosexual
rights? The bar wants to help, and its most elite members
want to help most of all. The whitest-shoe corporate law firms
will shower you with funding, provide million-dollar attorneys to sit on your board, and maybe even furnish a $600-an-
hour litigator to prosecute your case for free.

The bar has hardly forsworn its intimate relationship
with corporate America, of course. But even as it earns billions
of dollars a year in fees from its business clients, it pursues a
variety of causes that would have astounded the bar's early

172

leaders. It does so in the name of a venerable legal tradition: pro bono publico law, or legal service undertaken "for the public good." Pro bono publico law went through a radical transformation in the 1960s; ever since, it has been the vehicle through which elite corporate lawyers could participate in the entitlements revolution, in the litigation revolution that turned lawyers and judges into unelected legislators, and in the cultural revolution that turned America into a nation of victims.

The remaking of pro bono practice mirrors a transformation both of America's legal culture and of elite lawyers' self-understanding. When D.C. circuit judge Laurence Silberman entered Harvard Law School in 1958, he recalls, "practicing law itself was regarded as pro bono. Our professors thought the practice of law was an honorable and valuable calling." Today, Judge Silberman speculates, "lawyers see pro bono services as penance they pay for serving a capitalist system." Now the profession seems to find its ultimate justification in its feats of social engineering.

Formerly, generations of American lawyers understood their pro bono obligation—their obligation to serve the public good without pay—to mean ensuring the fair administration of justice. They helped courts as unpaid arbitrators and mediators and served on bar committees to improve the law. Equally important, they represented politically unpopular clients for free, to ensure justice for all. John Adams defended British soldiers accused of shooting Bostonians after the Battle of Bunker Hill; Algernon Sydney Sullivan, founder of the path-breaking Wall Street law firm Sullivan & Cromwell, represented Confederate sympathizers in New York. Less notoriously, small-town and country lawyers defended the local poor in criminal and civil courts without fee.

By the late nineteenth century, however, the traditional

informal mechanism for providing legal assistance to the poor no longer worked in the big industrial cities, with their teeming immigrant populations. In a small town, everyone—including the poor—knew who the local lawyer was and had access to him. Not so in the big cities, where lawyers were increasingly ensconced in large corporate law firms, serving the super-industrialists and their financiers. An immigrant factory hand would no sooner think of penetrating the downtown Beaux Arts fortresses of these new firms to ask for free legal help than of demanding a table at Delmonico's.

Yet even as lawyers became more specialized and remote, the legal needs of the urban poor were multiplying. Dishonest employers, sharpsters, and loan sharks preyed on the wage-earning multitudes. Contingency-fee lawyers might take on personal-injury claims, but they would have no interest in pursuing a small claim for uncollected wages. Unable to afford lawyers' retainers and court fees, and no longer able to knock on the local lawyer's door to ask for free representation, the urban poor were effectively shut out from justice.

Progressive reformers, fearing class warfare, set about devising new machinery to ensure universal access to the courts. In 1876, a group of prominent German-Americans in New York City created the first formal organization to dispense free legal assistance to the poor: the Deutsche Rechtsschutz Verein, or German Legal Aid Society. The organized bar had no part in the creation of this first Legal Aid Society; in fact, it was mildly hostile to a perceived competitor. But as similar societies sprang up across American cities, a lawyer's support for them, whether through money, direct services, or leadership, became an important means of fulfilling his pro bono publico duties.

From its inception, organized legal aid, consistent with Gilded Age philanthropic practice, unapologetically distinguished the deserving from the undeserving poor. The deserving poor were those who worked. The German Legal Aid Society's great early leader, Civil War veteran and elite New York lawyer Arthur von Briesen, declared: "Whoever receives our attention must show that he *has* rendered some service, that he has done some work, and that he is entitled to a corresponding consideration, which being denied we enforce in his behalf." The most frequent claim the early legal aid societies pursued was for uncollected wages. The non-working, long-term poor, whom today we would call the underclass, were outside the Society's ambit. So strong was the stigma against getting something for nothing that the New York Society began charging a fee of ten cents in 1896 for those able to pay, so that they would not feel they were receiving a handout.

Reginald Heber Smith's 1919 *Justice and the Poor* powerfully advanced the legal aid movement, spurring the legal profession to form twenty new legal aid societies in just two years, bringing the total to sixty-one. Carefully chronicling the continuing barriers to the courts faced by the poor, the Boston Brahmin lawyer concluded that America was betraying its commitment to equality before the law every day by pricing the poor out of justice.

What is most striking today in Smith's indictment of America's legal system is what he did not assert: he explicitly denied that the laws themselves discriminated against the poor. The problem lay solely in legal costs and procedural hurdles. Even here, Smith refused a class-warfare analysis. "No dominating group or class has consciously set out to foreclose the rights of the poor," he argued. The inherent conflict in society, Smith believed, was between the honest and the dishonest, not between the rich and the poor.

Like virtually all their peers, early legal aid practitioners

175

took for granted a distinction between courts and legislatures. The courts were for the adjudication of existing rights, they believed; reform of the laws, including reform to help the poor, took place in the legislature. They also assumed that legal aid was a private-sector obligation. When the National Lawyers Guild, a dissident group of liberal, radical, and communist attorneys, called for government-supported legal services in the early 1950s, an American Bar Association president responded with a consummate expression of the bar's conservatism. The "entry of the government into the field of providing legal services," he warned, "is too dangerous to be permitted to come about in our free America." Allow Washington to encroach, argued opponents of federally funded legal services, and you're paving the way to socialism.

A mere twenty years later, no bar leader would dare voice that opinion in polite company. None would defend the distinction between legislation and adjudication. What happened? The nation's massive culture change during the 1960s brought into currency a radically different philosophy of helping the poor, one that entailed a novel use of the courts. Once converted to the new view, the legal profession became among its most fervent evangelists.

During the War on Poverty, America jettisoned its traditional distinction between the deserving and the undeserving poor. It jettisoned as well traditional social work's effort to change self-destructive habits in the poor. Entitlements to government aid were the War on Poverty's panacea, and antipoverty warriors from the academic and legal left insisted that government help should be automatic and free of moralizing. The only criterion for receiving welfare should be economic need. A poor person who refused to labor had just as much claim to government money and services as someone struggling to work and support a family. After all, argued the War on Poverty's academic architects, American society was so unjust, so stacked against the poor, that judgment was unfair and individual behavior change useless. The poverty planners quickly enlisted the lawyers into the ranks of their entitlements revolution. Edgar Cahn, a civil rights strategist and speechwriter for Robert Kennedy, joined the new Office of Economic Opportunity, and persuaded this War on Poverty command center to create government-funded, "community-controlled" legal services to litigate the poor's grievances against society. It was a momentous development both for the legal profession and for American society as a whole.

The new, federally funded "legal services" agencies could not have been more different from the traditional voluntary legal aid societies—and over time they inexorably molded traditional legal aid into their exact image. The goal of the legal aid societies had been due-process justice: making sure that the poor have their day in court. The new legal services agencies had something quite different in mind: the redistribution of political and economic power. One legal services attorney described his work as "legal action designed to change the structure of the world in which poor people live."

Such high ambitions required scrapping centuries-old canons of professional ethics that forbade the solicitation of cases. Lawyers were supposed to wait for clients to come to them; if they were allowed to solicit clients, the reasoning went, they would foment unnecessary and destructive litigiousness. But the new legal services attorneys actively sought out cases as part of a political strategy, urged on by no less an authority than Attorney General Nicholas Katzenbach. "To be reduced to inaction by ethical inhibitions," Katzenbach announced, "is to let the canons of lawyers serve the cause of injustice." In time, the whole profession—most notoriously the plaintiffs' tort bar—would follow the lead of legal services attorneys and discard the inhibition against solicitation.

And how did the new legal services attorneys propose to "change the structure of the world"? By encouraging judges to create a whole new battery of rights. What was unfolding in the 1960s was nothing less than a reordering of government: a shifting of power from the legislature to the courts, with federally funded attorneys as the driving force. Nothing in the traditional legal aid movement anticipated this development.

Judge J. Skelly Wright of the D.C. Circuit Court of Appeals typified the new judicial activists. Wright created a novel body of tenants' rights out of whole cloth, by following, according to his own admission, his political convictions, not the law. In 1982, he reminisced: "I offer no apology for not following more closely the legal precedents which had cooperated in creating the conditions that I found unjust."

Though in reality the poor's demand for legal assistance had shrunk throughout the 1950s, legal services architects nevertheless tirelessly bemoaned a "crisis" in the legal needs of the poor. With breathtaking honesty, legal services founder Edgar Cahn explained the ruse. The legal services "crisis," he confessed, was wholly a product of the rights revolution currently under way. "Recent years have witnessed the creation of a vast and still growing array of legally vested rights," he wrote in 1968. "The developing case law regarding the rights of juveniles, of tenants in public housing, of welfare recipients, of persons accused of a crime, of minority group members, has challenged the capacity of the legal system. The sheer logistical dimension raised by the rights explosion poses a crisis to the law." Cahn was creating a self-generating machine. "The greater supply of legal services generates more rights, thereby generating more demand for services and bringing more grievances to the surface," he blithely announced.

This litigation machine behaved quite like an ATM. Earl Johnson, Jr., the Office of Economic Opportunity's former director of legal services, calculated in 1974 that liberalized welfare rules alone, the product of legal services litigation, had returned over $2 billion to welfare recipients in less than ten years. The desired redistribution of resources was under way. "A bare handful of lawyers," Johnson bragged, "has produced massive transfers of goods and services to the poor—some from the private sector and some from the public treasury."

At first, relations between the old-time legal aid society attorneys and the new government legal services crowd were testy. Advocates of government-funded legal services scorned their legal aid colleagues as too deferential to the bar and to legal traditions, and too paternalistic toward the poor. Many legal aid attorneys, for their part, warned that the new passion for "community control" was a destructive one. But even in the sixties, some legal aid offices started taking federal money; today, they are awash in it. As more and more legal aid societies jumped onto the bandwagon, they become indistinguishable from the legal services agencies in their agenda of maximizing entitlement use and multiplying rights.

Arthur von Briesen's and Reginald Heber Smith's quaint notion that workers deserve the most assistance disappeared overnight. The most significant rights being created were for non-workers: people on welfare. Legal services lawyers spurred the development of a new body of law for them: "poverty law," which was above all about maintaining an unimpeded stream of welfare benefits to recipients (though it included landlord-tenant and consumer law as well). Smith and von Briesen would have blanched at the notion that there should be a separate body of law for the poor—it was against

179

just such a possibility that they had fought so hard. But poverty law assumed that poor people are victims of systemic injustice that only lawyers could cure, primarily by suing the fast-multiplying government agencies that provide benefits to low-income people.

What was the bar's response to these momentous changes—changes that wholly redefined the role of lawyers in the American polity? Cautious at first, then rapturous. After some behind-the-scenes political maneuvering, the ABA discarded its long-standing opposition to federally supported legal services and never looked back. By 1981, when President Reagan tried to dismantle the Legal Services Corporation, on the grounds that its lawyers were engaging in rank politics with taxpayer money, it was the ABA's strenuous protest, above all, that saved the agency. The OEO's Earl Johnson, Jr., himself marveled at the "philosophical transformation" that overtook the establishment bar in the 1960s. The civil rights movement spurred that transformation as much as did the new legal services' success. Civil rights litigation was the great template for using the courts to change society, one with unimpeachable moral authority. Much subsequent rights litigation rode in on its coattails, though with far less justification. In its wake, lawyers lost their image as the great stuffed whales of American conservatism and became sex symbols, in the mold of attorneys general Robert Kennedy and Nicholas Katzenbach. Students clamored to get into law schools to join this new vanguard of social justice.

Once there, they often found the traditional study of law hazardous to their sensitive souls. One law student of the era whined that "law school teaches students to deal with every conceivable loss, that of an arm and leg, five dollars, a wife—every one, that is, but the most important, the loss of one's self." Law schools responded to such complaints by creating programs in poverty and civil rights law. Newly minted lawyers who joined firms demanded that their employers create official pro bono programs, so that they could participate in the rights revolution while pulling in large corporation-funded salaries. Elite law firms established pro bono community services departments to perform the same poverty law functions as the federal legal services offices. In this way, the legal services revolution had succeeded in redefining pro bono work in its image.

Starting in the 1970s, the ABA and local bar associations began furiously cranking out position papers on pro bono work and revising relevant codes of professional responsibility to further the bar's involvement in the advocacy agenda. Over a decade ago, the Ford Foundation created the ABA's Law Firm Pro Bono Project, which pressures elite firms to commit 3 to 5 percent of their total billable hours to hands-on pro bono work, in addition to donating money to legal groups that represent the poor. The pressure has been effective. Many large firms now have full-time pro bono coordinators or partners, complete with staff; almost as many regularly place associates with advocacy and legal services groups on a rotating basis. The organized bars and the advocacy groups together have created an elaborate infrastructure to link big firms with the ever-proliferating public interest law outfits.

This infrastructure urges firms to take on big, politically charged cases. The results: in just the last several years, titans of the corporate bar have sued to dissolve anti-gang injunctions in gang-infested southern California areas; to fight quality-of-life law enforcement in San Francisco; to saddle prisons with court orders; to allow felons to vote; to block the death penalty in hundreds of cases, including for a woman who kidnapped and sexually abused a thirteen-year-old girl, injected the girl with drain cleaner, then shot her in the back when she didn't die; to force gun manufacturers to pay potentially millions in damages to crime victims; to defend minority set-asides and preferential admissions policies; to require bilingual education for Haitians; to make the Virginia Military Institute and the Citadel admit girl cadets; to declare the busty waitresses at the Hooters restaurant chain victims of gender discrimination; to compel the Boy Scouts to accept homosexual scoutmasters; to block the classification of AIDS as a sexually transmitted, or even communicable, disease; to enact homosexual marriage; and to challenge industrial facilities on grounds of "environmental racism." In New York City alone, big-firm panjandrums have sued to force the city to pay union-scale wages to workfare workers; to enjoin aggressive crime-fighting in high-crime neighborhoods; to force the city to spend even more on the HIV-infected than the mind-boggling amount it already disburses; to wring $600 million from the city in a sex discrimination case (successfully prosecuted); to require the Saint Patrick's Day Parade to accept homosexual-rights marchers; and to force New York City to create special foster-care programs for children who "question their sexuality." And this is just a sampling of cases undertaken in the name of the public good.

Recall that pro bono work gave New York City its unique, and uniquely tortured, court-ordered homeless system. It took shape when Sullivan & Cromwell associate Robert Hayes filed a massive pro bono suit claiming the city had a constitutional duty to provide shelter on demand. The city eventually settled the suit on terms agreeable to Hayes, terms that included court oversight of its every move regarding the homeless. It has never been free of homeless litigation since. When Hayes left Sullivan & Cromwell to found the Coalition for the Homeless, where he continued his nonstop suits against the city, he by no means sacrificed the unparalleled resources of New York's elite firms. The "trick" of the Coalition, he explains, "was to have a half-dozen cases going at any given time, all class actions, always co-counseled by major firms." Maria Foscarinis, director of the high-profile National Law Center on Homelessness and Poverty, replicated the same "trick" with power firms in Washington, D.C., Hayes observes.

Hayes has used Paul, Weiss, Rifkind, Wharton & Garrison; Cahill Gordon & Reindel; Cravath, Swaine & Moore; and Davis Polk & Wardwell. Steven Banks of the Legal Aid Society, currently the main homeless-rights litigator in the city, has relied on Debevoise & Plimpton; Sullivan & Cromwell; and Winthrop, Stimson, Putnam & Roberts. Besides providing actual manpower, Manhattan's firms have poured millions of dollars into the incessant homelessness suits through contributions to the Legal Aid Society, the Coalition for the Homeless, the Urban Justice Center, and the ACT-UP spin-off, Housing Works.

I asked Robert Hayes why he didn't take his case for shelter on demand to the legislature, where it belongs. "Personally, I don't like politics," he replied forthrightly. "It's really hard."

Here, in just eight frank words, is the trouble with class-action and other litigation that seeks to create new rights—the very heart of contemporary pro bono publico work. Hayes is right: persuading a legislature to commit the billions that New York City has been forced to spend in irrational ways on the homeless would be a whole lot harder than persuading one judge to order those billions spent. The legislature has to balance competing demands for taxpayer dollars; a judge can order an elaborate shelter and housing system without having to trade off dollars for teachers, say, versus dollars for private apartments for drug addicts with AIDS. Big political litigation allows elite lawyers to make an end run around the political process.

And, in so doing, they make others pay for their vision of

the world, notes Francis Menton, Jr., a partner at Willkie Farr & Gallagher. Menton has long observed the nexus between elite firms and the advocacy groups they support through pro bono lawyering and contributions. "Millionaire attorneys have decided how society should work," he says, "and they use the courts to make the middle class pay for their schemes." Menton calls the Legal Aid Society, now wholly transformed from its sober origins, an "agent of millionaire attorneys for forcing their charitable preferences on middle-class taxpayers."

Indeed, there is a breezy indifference among the Society's supporters to the costs of Legal Aid's demands. Over the years, for example, the city has paid out $5 million in court-ordered fines to single mothers claiming homelessness. Each mother got a $250 windfall if, instead of being placed immediately in housing, she had to stay overnight with her children in the homeless intake center. If she stayed a second night, she got another $250, and so on. I asked Cleary, Gottlieb, Steen & Hamilton partner Mitch Lowenthal, who has participated in the ongoing homeless litigation against the city, if this wasn't an irrational use of funds. Wouldn't the $5 million in fines be better spent for housing than for overcompensating a minor inconvenience that ordinary travelers must put up with often enough? Lowenthal was blasé: "How much is $5 million compared with the city budget?" he responded rhetorically. To a Cleary partner (1998 per-partner profits: $1 million), $5 million may seem like pocket change, but to the majority of city taxpayers, it's real money.

Pro bono work provides many other opportunities for showering taxpayer dollars on favorite charities. To understand how this works, first jettison the biggest misconception about contemporary pro bono litigation: that it is done for free. In fact, firms purporting to be fulfilling their public service obligations sometimes rake in thousands, even millions, of dollars in fees, usually from the government. The firms cash in under statutes that allow winning plaintiffs in rights cases to collect their attorneys' fees from the defendant (though the rationale that firms wouldn't otherwise take such cases breaks down in a pro bono context). The Silicon Valley powerhouse firm of Wilson Sonsini Goodrich & Rosati demanded $8.3 million in fees from defendant California in a prison litigation suit, then magnanimously settled for $3.5 million. San Francisco's Morrison & Foerster collected $1.24 million from California for invalidating a parental notification requirement for minors seeking abortions.

Having collected fees for something they claim to be doing charitably, a remarkable 30 percent of big firms pocket the entire sum without apology. The rest make an enormous show of donating some or all of the money—fresh from taxpayers' pockets—to their favorite public interest group. Often the recipient is the very advocacy group with which the firm just co-litigated, and the money goes to finance more suits against the public treasury. Thus is the litigation machine kept ever stoked with taxpayer dollars.

New York City has just witnessed precisely such a taxpayer-fleecing operation. Cahill Gordon and Schulte Roth & Zabel teamed up with Marcia Lowery, an attorney who sues child welfare agencies for a living as head of Children's Rights, Inc., to try to put New York City's entire child welfare administration under court supervision. They filed their suit just as Commissioner Nicholas Scoppetta began sweeping reforms in the agency. Commissioner Scoppetta immediately proposed a settlement. No go, declared Lowery, and proceeded to ring up nearly $11 million in pre-trial costs, calculated at corporate rates of up to $515 an hour. Almost four years later, the parties settled, on terms almost identical to what Commissioner Scoppetta had initially proposed. Those terms involved nothing the city was not already doing.

Now Lowery and Schulte Roth are asking the city for $9.18 million in fees. Cahill Gordon has already collected $1.57 million from New York State, also a party in the suit; it handed the $1.57 million, minus its expenses, right back to Lowery for more litigation. David Brodsky, the former Schulte Roth partner in charge of the litigation, will not return phone calls about the case; the firm has not yet announced what it intends to do with its expected $1.4 million. Perhaps it could first poll the city's taxpayers, to see how they would like their money spent. Many big-firm lawyers today sound like Marxist academics when they discuss pro bono work. Take John Kiernan, a $600-an-hour litigation partner at Debevoise & Plimpton, who is also director of Legal Services for New York and the Lawyers Committee for Civil Rights Under the Law. Scorning the homely small-town tradition of pro bono work, he defines pro bono for "us big-city litigators" as the "process of committing resources for the legal representation of the disenfranchised." "Disenfranchised" is pretty strong stuff, calling up images of a racist South trampling on voting rights. Asked for an example of the disenfranchised today, Kiernan cites blacks allegedly targeted by the New York City police for stop-and-frisks. Are their legislators not representing them? "I mean disempowered, not disenfranchised literally," he says.

But disempowered? Consider that Kiernan's firm, spurred on by the Amadou Diallo shooting, is suing the New York City Police Department, charging that its Street Crimes Unit illegally singles out blacks for street stops. In the wake of that shooting, black leaders in New York City and beyond focused unprecedented international attention on the NYPD; they persuaded the president, the First Lady, the Justice Department, the U.S. Civil Rights Commission, the New York attorney general, and a host of lesser political entities to denounce the department. Given that political muscle, it strains credulity to claim that blacks in Harlem and the Bronx lack political power.

But wait, there is one group that is literally disenfranchised today—felons—and Debevoise & Plimpton has sued to change that, too. Kiernan claims that the law that disenfranchises felons violates blacks' voting rights, because so many blacks are in prison. Kiernan has no problem taking away white felons' voting rights, but "you worry when [the disenfranchisement laws] have a racial impact." Isn't the real problem the black crime rate? No, because the drug sentencing laws discriminate, too, he says—a dodge that ignores the very real problem of crime and violence in minority neighborhoods.

Progressives once denounced the corporate bar for its stuffy self-certainty. Today's elite bar possesses the same self-confidence, but it directs its infallibility at different targets. Milbank, Tweed, Hadley & McCloy partner Joseph Genova, for example, head of the firm's pro bono program, passionately opposes welfare reform, which he calls a "diabolical scheme" to "shove as many people from the rolls as possible [and] remove the tax burden from the wealthy." The previous welfare regime seems pretty much fine to him. But what about the harsh criticism that people in poor communities, especially the working poor, make of that regime? "I'm aware of the phenomenon," he says. "I'm confident that the complainers don't know what they're talking about." One can't help think that residents of welfare-saturated neighborhoods might have a better idea of welfare's effects than a Milbank partner (1998 per-partner profits: $1.1 million), however.

Fortunately, pro bono work has broadened in the last several years beyond adversarial suits against government and claims of discrimination. Now, corporate attorneys from Paul Weiss and Winthrop Stimson, among other firms, help small businesses, many of them located in minority areas or empowerment zones, with their legal needs. Milbank Tweed lawyers counsel individuals seeking to adopt children and help elderly homeowners trapped in foreclosure proceedings. Cleary Gottlieb attorneys mentor inner-city high school students. The Volunteers of Legal Services, a New York City pro bono clearinghouse, finds attorneys for poor elderly people needing legal help. There has even been a slight countermovement to include more "conservative" cases in support of personal responsibility, assimilation, and color-blindness. In a landmark for conservative pro bono work, Los Angeles–based Gibson, Dunn & Crutcher represented Cheryl Hopwood in her successful challenge to racial preferences at the University of Texas Law School. Davis Polk has defended the eviction of drug dealers from public housing and recently supported a family member's request to medicate a severely psychotic sibling without her consent. Skadden, Arps, Slate, Meagher & Flom defended California's ballot initiative banning bilingual education against a court challenge, albeit anonymously.

Still, at least Skadden Arps took the case—unlike the prestigious Manhattan firm where two partners wanted to argue against racial gerrymandering several years ago, also without using their firm's name on the legal papers. They were forbidden, on the grounds that fighting for color-blind legislative districting would tar the firm as "racist" at law schools. "I became discouraged," one of the partners recalls. "To take a high-profile conservative case—too many people here think it's disgusting."

Overall, getting prestigious firms to accept conservative cases pro bono remains an uphill struggle. Top-scoring Chinese-American students, barred by racial quotas from San Francisco's prestigious Lowell High School, were turned away by every big San Francisco firm they solicited for pro bono representation. Dennis Saffran of the mildly conservative Center for the Community Interest, an advocate for public safety and quality of life, says that finding pro bono counsel for every case is "a fight." By contrast, when the ABA sent out a call for additional firms to represent homosexual scoutmaster James Dale against the Boy Scouts, Morrison & Foerster's pro bono coordinator Kathi Pugh had a Mo Foe attorney lined up "within an hour," she says. Other firms, such as Kramer Levin Naftalis & Frankel, signed up as well.

It is time for firms to ask whether their pro bono programs in fact serve the public good. The problems of the long-term poor today cannot be solved with litigation; attorneys would accomplish far more acting as Big Brothers and Big Sisters, scoutmasters, and tutors. Though the pro bono industry pushes for bigger and bigger cases, what the most troubled poor need is on the micro level—an understanding of work, the commitment to stay in school, a stable family. If benefits and more government spending could solve juvenile delinquency, non-work, or illegitimacy, we would have solved them long ago.

Since the 1960s, many lawyers have believed they are specifically fitted to improve society by creating new rights that a heartless majority refuses to recognize. The pro bono docket exemplifies this newfound hubris. Its failure to bring about any visible improvement should inspire humility.

[2000]

SOL STERN

How Businessmen Shouldn't Help the Schools

ON APRIL 29 I became a New York City "Principal for a Day," along with about one thousand of the city's business executives, a dozen or so local politicians, and such luminaries as bad-boy actor Billy Baldwin, Diane von Furstenberg, Norma Kamali, and First Lady Hillary Clinton. With two children of my own in city schools, I had become intrigued with this highly regarded program, which attempts to improve public schools by linking them with private-sector companies and managers. I even dared to hope that the executives who became Principals for a Day might be able to spur the public schools into becoming more innovative and productive.

190

I found, alas, that the businessmen left their managerial street smarts in the office, wasting a golden opportunity for reform. They came to their schools with the best intentions and bearing gifts, yet unwittingly they conspired in propping up an indefensible, failing system.

The guiding genius behind Principal for a Day is thirty-six-year-old Lisa Belzberg, daughter of one of Canada's richest families and wife of Matthew Bronfman, son of Canadian tycoon Edgar Bronfman. Attractive and articulate, with degrees from Barnard College and the London School of Economics, Belzberg worked for political campaign consultant David Garth and then became producer of the Charlie Rose TV talk show. She moves easily among the city's movers and shakers; her name on an invitation draws willing supporters to the program.

After serving as a Principal for a Day five years ago, when the program was still small and run entirely by the Board of Education, Belzberg found a cause. She created Pencil (Public Education Needs Civic Involvement in Learning) as a not-for-profit organization with thirteen employees and a half-million-dollar budget. Pencil took over the struggling program and expanded it into the largest and most successful operation of its kind in the country.

Belzberg sends her own children to an exclusive Jewish day school but bubbles with enthusiasm about the public schools. "I truly believe in the notion of public education in this country," she told me. "It is the one place where everyone can be accepted. There are beautiful things going on in the system. . . . I believe that by putting the private sector into the schools, we are bringing the city together."

In the past few years, companies such as NBC, Primedia, and HBO have poured millions of dollars' worth of computers, books, and furniture into their assigned schools through

191

What Makes Charity Work?

Principal for a Day—as well as offering students a host of internships and tutoring programs. While these gifts are undoubtedly useful to the individual schools that receive them, there is little evidence that Principal for a Day has brought about any systemic school improvement.

But the program has brought about a bonanza of glowing publicity for the public school system. For years I found myself bemused by the gushing columns by journalists from all four major New York dailies about their Principal for a Day stints. Somehow, none of these normally skeptical writers ever seemed to visit a poorly performing school or to serve with a less than stellar principal or to observe a lazy teacher. This year, the favorable media buzz began even before we honorary principals were sent off on our assignments. A *New York* magazine profile depicted Belzberg as an angel of mercy, mobilizing private-sector relief for the city's worthy but allegedly underfunded schools. The magazine favorably contrasted her efforts to the sinister influence of billionaire investor Ted Forstmann ("a friend of Newt Gingrich"), who had just raised $170 million for private school scholarships—privately funded vouchers—to allow forty thousand poor children to escape failing public schools nationwide. "Under the guise of fair competition, Forstmann is abandoning public education," the magazine intoned. The article failed to note that Principal for a Day was honoring *New York* magazine's owner, Primedia, for its donations of books to the public schools.

Even if you believe the dubious proposition that providing private scholarships to thousands of poor kids trapped in failing public schools is the equivalent of "abandoning" public education, that leaves unanswered this key question: What should business leaders be doing if they really want to help save public education? Is donating books and computers the answer?

I was assigned to I.S. 59, a junior high school in Spring-

192

field Gardens, Queens, a solidly middle- and working-class black neighborhood near the Nassau County border. Surrounding the vast rectangular school building are small one-family homes with neatly kept lawns. The building houses over fifteen hundred students, virtually all of them black, most from intact families, and comparatively few who are in poverty.

When I called the principal, Antonio K'tori, to arrange my visit, I could sense his disappointment in getting a writer rather than a businessman. "What can you do for us?" he asked in a somewhat forlorn voice.

Thrown off guard, I replied, with a chuckle, "Maybe I could fire some of your teachers."

K'tori took it in good humor. He told me that he had only a handful of below-par teachers, because over the past several years he had forced several others—by methods unspecified—to transfer or retire. This led us to the constraints the teachers' union contract places on the school principal's managerial autonomy. K'tori told me that, despite the contract's well-known restrictions, he felt he could run a successful school.

K'tori, thirty-eight, grew up in England, the son of Sudanese parents. Short, trim, and impeccably dressed, with an authoritative, no-nonsense manner, he starts off each day with a personal message piped over the school's intercom system into every classroom. The day I visited, the morning ritual began with the Pledge of Allegiance. Then K'tori called for a "moment of reflection," followed by a short pep talk about how important it was for students to study hard for their upcoming tests.

Following the same six-hour routine that most Principals for a Day go through, I was introduced to the students over the intercom, and then I offered a few words of encouragement. I sat in the principal's office with K'tori as he handled discipline issues with several students and their parents. I visited several classes, had lunch in the school cafeteria, and spoke at a career class about journalism as a profession. I couldn't shower the school with computers or books, but K'tori did ask that I write a positive story.

In truth, I found much that was positive, sometimes even inspirational, about I.S. 59. First, notwithstanding a few progressive-education platitudes, K'tori is basically a traditionalist. He imposes a dress code, he says, "because it takes the children away from the feeling that school is unimportant and that they can get here any way they please." All of his math and science classes are tracked for ability. He believes in high standards and thinks that his children should be able to pass the state- and citywide tests. He is usually in the building by 6 a.m. and often stays well past 8 p.m. every day. "The school is his life," one of his secretaries told me. Why does he do it? "Because education is the most important gift I can supply to these children," he told me.

According to Board of Education test statistics, K'tori's incessant prodding of his students and staff about academic achievement pays off. In 1998, 57 percent of his students scored at or above grade level in the citywide reading test, compared with 49.8 percent of students in schools with students from similar socioeconomic backgrounds. In math, I.S. 59 scored 66.9 percent, compared with 61.6 percent for similar schools. Moreover, a significant number of the students are doing accelerated work. Almost 20 percent of I.S. 59's eighth-graders take and pass the difficult Sequential 1 mathematics and earth-science Regents tests, normally given in high school.

By chance, I wandered into an advanced seventh-grade science class and watched John Como, twenty-nine, teach a magnificent lesson on human genetics and DNA. The thirty-five students—all black, all wearing neat school uniforms—

were totally enrapt, answering Como's probing questions and asking intelligent questions of their own. Here was a scene, I thought, that certainly confirmed Lisa Belzberg's insistence that "beautiful things" are happening in the city's schools and that more New Yorkers should be made aware of that fact.

Just as certainly, however, Como's employment status is an indictment of the system's dysfunctional personnel policies—and New Yorkers should know about that, too. After high school on Long Island, Como enlisted in the navy and served on an attack submarine during the Gulf War. He then went to Tulane on an ROTC scholarship, graduating with a B.S. in molecular and cell biology. Returning to the New York area, he turned down the opportunity to work in industry and opted to try teaching for a while. The Board of Ed granted him a temporary license, provided that he go back to school and take twelve education credits within the next three years. Then he'd have to earn a master's degree in education to become permanently certified.

Anyone who walks into Como's classroom could testify that he is already a master teacher. With his military background, his knowledge of a difficult academic subject, and his energy in the classroom, Como should be worth his weight in gold to any school. Yet despite his three stellar years in the classroom, the city and state education bureaucracies are still hounding him to complete this or that education course and go through a seemingly endless maze to get his permanent teaching credential, exemplifying the public education system's absurd credentialism. So despite his talent, Como is mired at the bottom of the salary scale, earning about $32,000 per year. Out of that munificent sum, he has to fork over $600 per year (after taxes) in compulsory union dues and then thousands more on his education courses and on various fees to the state to process his license applications. For the time being, he told me, he gets "a great deal of satisfaction" from his job and will stay on. For the long term, he says, "I don't know what I am going to do."

After leaving Como's classroom, I struck up a conversation in the hallway with a math teacher with graying hair, who identified himself as "Mr. Denmark—like the country." He had been at the school for more than thirty years and seemed embittered with the school system as well as with his own union leadership for accepting a contract with insufficient raises. Without embarrassment, he told me that, since the city didn't show any appreciation for teachers, he had decided that he would work to the contractual minimum (six hours and twenty minutes a day) in return for his nearly $70,000 salary. His tenure protection means that, as long as he meets his assigned classes for forty-two minutes and does a reasonable job of keeping to the prescribed curriculum, there's not much that his principal or anyone else can do about it.

Even more perversely, despite Principal K'tori's enormous responsibility and 80- to 90-hour workweek, his annual compensation is only a few thousand dollars more than Mr. Denmark's. He's probably earning about $20 per hour—and that's for running a $9 million enterprise with 140 employees. We should celebrate K'tori's dedication and idealism—but this is not the way to build a system that attracts excellent school leaders. Little wonder that the city is losing some of its best principals to the suburbs. Mayor Giuliani has offered raises of nearly $30,000 in return for the principals' giving up tenure and accepting that, as managers, they should work under contracts renewable on the basis of their performance. So far, however, the principals' union has rejected this offer, holding fast to the prevailing public school culture of protecting jobs rather than accepting accountability.

Near the end of the day, I spent a final few minutes with Principal K'tori. There wasn't time to discuss all my impressions, so I returned to his very first question when we spoke by telephone a week earlier. I asked him to name the one thing *he* would ask for if he had a Principal for a Day with the power to grant his wish. He'd request money for an after-school remedial program for the under-performing students in the school, he said.

This was an excellent choice and reflected K'tori's educational values. Despite I.S. 59's overall good numbers on standardized tests, too many of its students remain way behind in crucial academic skills. More important than new computers or other hardware, K'tori recognized, nothing would be as valuable to his at-risk children as extra time with a talented and productive teacher.

Still, if I could wave a magic wand, it's not the gift that I would offer. Instead, I would grant K'tori the authority to control his own budget and his staff. On the books, I.S. 59 spends about $9 million per year; but it is the central Board of Education, not K'tori, that allocates those dollars to the various school functions—making our school system one of the last examples of a command-and-control economy since the Berlin Wall fell. Board bureaucrats get to decide that I.S. 59 will have so many teacher and assistant-principal positions, so many cafeteria workers, so many clerks and secretaries, so many security guards, and so many custodial workers. If, instead, Principal K'tori could decide on the most efficient allocation of staff and resources, he could easily find a way to pay for that extra remediation. To put it another way, were public education a rationally managed enterprise, K'tori would have the authority to allocate the school's resources and staff to accomplish his educational mission, rather than have the central authority's bureaucratic rules subvert that mission. Private school principals enjoy just such discretion—one reason that their schools are almost always more cost-effective and productive than public schools.

As I left I.S. 59 and drove back to Manhattan, I wondered

why the business executives who served as Principals for a Day were either unable or reluctant to grasp this fundamental management issue—the bedrock principle of their own professional lives. I was soon to get an answer.

My visit to I.S. 59 turned out to be only the first part of the program, and perhaps not its most important part. After the school bell rings, the Principals for a Day, plus many of the real principals, gather for a town-hall meeting and awards ceremony. Two years ago *New York Times* publisher Arthur Sulzberger Jr. hosted the event in the *Times* building. This year, with the number of participants swelling to more than eleven hundred, the event took place in a large, ornate hall at the New York Public Library.

There was a special irony in that choice of venue. Eight days earlier, in the same hall, Ted Forstmann's Children's Scholarship Fund had staged its own gala to celebrate the granting of its 40,000 scholarships to poor public school kids. I had attended the Forstmann event, and the comments of Andrew Young and Martin Luther King III at that ceremony still reverberated in my mind. The two civil-rights leaders had pleaded for a new civil-rights agenda for the twenty-first century—the right of poor minority children to be able to choose a school that really would educate them. Another theme, sounded by Mayor Rudy Giuliani and Forstmann himself, was that when public schools have to compete with private schools for students, they tend to get better, so that vouchers ultimately improve public education, not "abandon" it. In his remarks, Mayor Giuliani had stressed that 168,000 poor New York City families with kids in the public schools—fully one-third of all those eligible—had applied for the Forstmann scholarships, an astonishing indictment of the existing system.

I hardly expected to find much support at the Principals for a Day gala for using vouchers to spur competition in education. Still, I did wonder if any of the business executives had taken note of the Soviet-style workplace practices in the schools they visited. Before the ceremony, I found myself in a seat next to a Principal for a Day named Amy Larkin, president of a consulting company that puts together private/ public ventures. She told me that she'd been assigned to an elementary school in Brooklyn with a new young principal, who was being sabotaged by the old-guard clerical and secretarial staff. She was surprised to learn that the secretaries and clerks—just like the teachers—were covered by rigid civil service and union protections and couldn't be fired or transferred. At that point a woman nearby, who identified herself as a real elementary-school principal from District 2 in Manhattan, said that every new principal had to figure out how to come to terms with her clerical staff. The principal then confided that her own school secretary was seventy years old, had Alzheimer's disease, and couldn't remember anything she was told.

Any hope that the Principals for a Day would get to air these issues quickly evaporated. It became clear that this event was part political rally and part revival meeting to drum up support for the New York City education system as it is, and for the people who run it. Seated in the first two rows of honor were Chancellor Rudy Crew, Board of Education president William Thompson, United Federation of Teachers president Randi Weingarten, and principals' union president Donald Singer. Sprinkled among them were the eager politicians— including Mark Green and Fernando Ferrer—who hanker to run for higher office as candidates of the no-change-in-education interests. Next to Chancellor Crew was Hillary Clinton, also primed to run for political office in New York as the anointed candidate of the same public education establishment.

Casual and elegant, Lisa Belzberg opened the meeting by asking everyone to pull together to "combat negative perceptions of the system." Without explaining what was so positive about the system, she went on to say that "long after vouchers and charters and Rudy versus Rudy, Chase Manhattan will still be there, and so will our schools, and we will still have the responsibility of educating our children for the workforce." She then turned the microphone over to Charlie Rose and sat down at the front of the stage, her legs draped over the edge.

"All of you have had a remarkable experience," said Rose, who surely does these events better than anyone else in the world. "We now want to hear what happened to you today." Rose then worked the crowd, offering the mike to anyone who wanted to stand up and speak.

Larry Greengrass, a senior partner in the law firm of Mound, Cotton, and Wollan, recounted his visit to P.S. 176 in Bay Ridge, Brooklyn, where, he said, he was thrilled to find a huge banner welcoming him, and where the "entire fifth grade" put on a performance for him. "The most amazing part of the day," he said, occurred when he sat in on a conference about a pupil who may have been the victim of abuse. "It was inspiring to me that there were all those professionals working so hard to help one kid," he said.

Jolie Schwab, a senior general attorney for ABC, spoke of the "dedicated and talented" teachers at the junior high school she had visited. She then addressed Chancellor Crew directly, concerned that "our teachers were leaving for the suburbs." Union boss Weingarten nodded approvingly as Crew stood up and took the mike. "What you saw," Crew told Schwab, "is what it is like every day. And it's true that our teachers are being cherry-picked by the suburbs. We have become a training ground for teachers for the suburbs." In fact, no hard evidence exists that teachers are stampeding to the suburbs. Nevertheless, Crew went on, to prevent this calamity, the teachers had to get the salaries they deserved. The audience broke into applause.

Not to be upstaged, principals' union chief Donald Singer stood up to say that the city's talented principals were also leaving for the suburbs. Turning directly to Crew, he urged: "Let's get a contract [for the principals] now." More applause. The same executives, of course, would have laughed instead of clapping, if someone had proposed that because they were losing some talented middle managers to a competitor, they should give equal raises to each and every one of their managers, regardless of merit.

After another honorary principal recounted how nervous she'd been to get on her school's elevator with two of its minority students until they expressed their friendliness, Strauss Zelnick, the CEO of B.M.G. Entertainment, told of his visit to Midwood High School in Brooklyn and of the difficulties its principal was having keeping up the maintenance of his grand old building. Zelnick announced that he had committed $25,000 of his company's resources to help out. "We used to build beautiful schools in this city," Zelnick said. "It's time to say to the federal government and the state: Why don't you start putting up some money?" More applause. Everyone in the room seemed to have erased from his memory bank the fact that hundreds of millions of dollars of school construction money had disappeared into a dark hole because of the featherbedding work rules and rank incompetence at the Board of Education's School Construction Authority. Instead of trying to figure out how to eliminate the operatically flamboyant waste that virtually defines the system, the assembled business executives, despite their M.B.A.s and years of real-world experience, were applauding a proposal to keep shoveling money to the very people responsible for the failure. Only in public education.

Inevitably, Charlie Rose turned the mike over to the First Lady. She told us of her visit to I.S. 226 in Queens, where, characteristically, she conducted her own little town-hall meeting

201

with some of the students. "It was interesting to hear the students talk about how they are always stereotyped," she said, leading her to remark, somewhat vaguely, that we all "have a lot of stereotypes about public schools." In a preview of what looks likely to be one of her Senate campaign themes against Mayor Giuliani, she said, "Let's not scapegoat and point fingers at an entire system." She then went into high policy mode: we can't improve the public schools without new money for "reducing classroom size" and for "new facilities," she said. Touting her husband's plan to spend federal dollars to hire 100,000 more teachers, she compared it to the Clinton administration's successful effort to put more cops on the street. "If you have more police, you have a better chance of reducing crime. If you have more teachers, you can do a better job of teaching the students," she remarked, ignoring the fact that more cops on the street didn't get results until they were properly managed.

It went on like this for forty minutes, as one after another of these highly successful men and women stood up and heaped praise on the "hardworking" and "dedicated" people who were doing such a "great" job educating our children. Were they talking about the same school system that I have gotten to know so well? The system that virtually guarantees lifetime jobs for all its teachers and principals, regardless of how little or how much they work? The system in which fewer than half the children who enter high school manage to graduate in four years? The system that, year after year, has almost one hundred schools on the State Education Department's Schools Under Registration Review failure list? The system in which two-thirds—67 percent—of all fourth-graders can't pass a very basic reading test administered by the state?

After the meeting, Donald Singer of the principals' union told me that "you can't apply the principles of marketplace competition to the schools, because education is not a business." Of course he believes that: his union exists to shield members from the risks of the marketplace. But why do so many Principals for a Day also accept it? I was dumbfounded that these shrewd, talented business people, some of whom manage the most entrepreneurial and competitive companies in the world and rightly boast that they can manage *anything* efficiently, would willingly draw down an iron curtain of denial when it came to the enterprise of public education.

In a more personal way, I was also angry. Few of the executives who were gushing about the schools they visited would actually consider sending their own children there, just as Hillary Clinton wouldn't send her daughter to the Washington, D.C., public schools that she says shouldn't be "scapegoated" and "stereotyped." They seemed to be saying that the public schools were doing an excellent job for other people's children. As one of those other people, I resented being told that the quality of the education my children were receiving is good enough, when it isn't. I also knew that the fault in my kids' schooling had nothing to do with a shortage of computers, the size of their classes, or lack of funds. After all, next year the city will spend some $10.1 billion on the schools— averaging out to around $9,200 per pupil—and a good part of that will be wasted.

I don't begrudge these executives the extra money they spend on their children's private school education. What I want for my children's schools has nothing to do with money. I want a system based on the fundamental idea that the interests of schoolchildren come first, ahead of the interests of the system's employees, with their lifetime job security. Even in just a five- or six-hour day in the public schools, any Principal for a Day who'd taken Management 101 should have been able to figure this one out.

A few days later, I telephoned a handful of the Principals for a Day—among them a senior manager at American Express, a vice president of Goldman Sachs, and a senior vice president of Home Box Office. Clearly, they had volunteered for the program out of decent motives and genuine concern about the city's future. Clearly, too, one of the reasons they had been so impressed by what they saw was that their expectations had been so low. When I asked if they were disturbed that, because of the union contract, it was practically impossible to fire an incompetent teacher or even check on a teacher's productivity, several responded that of course it troubled them. But, they said, they didn't feel they knew enough about such issues to speak out publicly. In response to my suggestion that the public schools could be improved if they followed more competitive, market-driven personnel policies, Richard Plepler, the HBO v.p., said, "I simply do not have good enough baseline information to make a judgment like that." Yet Plepler, who identified himself as a friend of Lisa Belzberg's, didn't hesitate to make the judgment that more money for higher teacher salaries and smaller classes would improve the public schools.

In our discussion after the town-hall meeting, Belzberg told me, "I am not in the business of trying to reform the system." On the contrary, she envisions the (by now) thousands of business executives who have participated in Principal for a Day and "who have influence in this city" becoming a force to help persuade elected officials to pour ever more resources into the existing public school system. She cited two examples in which some of the Principals for a Day had already tried to exercise such influence: the school construction bond act that was on the state ballot two years ago but failed to get a majority of the voters, and the school governance bill that passed the State Legislature two years ago, essentially recentralizing the school system and giving Chancellor Crew expanded new powers—with results that are hard to cheer.

For all her enthusiasm and goodwill, Belzberg's priorities

are upside down. Business executives are better off allowing the education establishment and the unions to fight their own battles in Albany for more money and power—something they excel at anyway. As for the Principal for a Day program, let businessmen be businessmen. The business community should prod the public schools to change their dysfunctional workplace habits. The executives should bring to the schools the same unsentimental management hardheadedness that has made American enterprises the envy of the world. Who, more than a businessman, has the authority to say that no enterprise can prosper that doesn't hold individuals accountable, rewarding merit and punishing failure, keeping everybody's attention focused on results, recognizing that employees can't flourish unless customers do, and giving managers the authority and responsibility for making their operations succeed? Who understands better than a businessman that centralized, top-down management bureaucracies belong to the days of tail fins, not e-mail? Businessmen shouldn't be embarrassed to judge the schools by the same standards that make them successful in their own companies—and to insist, as Principals for a Day, that their tax dollars get spent with the same efficiency as their investment dollars.

One can almost hear the unions sputtering in protest. No, of course this doesn't mean that the public schools should be turned into profit-making enterprises. What it does mean is that the system should be managed with one preeminent goal in mind—to get the most out of every tax dollar spent on the schools and to get an effective teacher into every classroom. With their foot already in the schoolhouse door, and their bona fides as generous public school supporters established, the Principals for a Day could press the system to contract out some functions (such as lunch and custodial services) by competitive bidding in order to save money for the classroom. Instead of seeing more and more taxpayer funds wasted on school construction boondoggles, the business executives could develop innovative proposals for bringing in the private sector to build and maintain school buildings. They could map out an incentive-laden personnel system that would reward productive employees and weed out malingerers. They could help convince Chancellor Crew that the best way to keep his high-performing principals from leaving is, first, to allow them to control their schools and, second, to reward them with bonuses for improving their kids' academic performance. The executives could even lobby the Board of Education to hang tough with the teachers' union next year and negotiate a labor contract that monitors teacher productivity, a contract that finally helps children more than it coddles nonperforming teachers.

If the Principals for a Day could persuade the powers that be to try some or all of these elementary business practices, they might actually help save public education in this city. If they don't, if they continue to insist that they are not "in the business of reform," they will become increasingly irrelevant to the 1.1 million children who presently have no choice but to rely on the public schools as they are. As we used to say in the sixties, if you're not part of the solution, you're part of the problem.

[1999]

Sol Stern

Who Says the Homeless Should Work?

THE POLITICAL ARGUMENTS often get testy on New York One's popular evening TV talk-fest, *The Road to City Hall*. But it's hard to remember anything quite like the recent confrontation between George McDonald and Steven Banks, two of the founding fathers of the city's homeless-rights movement. McDonald instantly went on the attack, accusing the city's oldest homeless-advocacy group, the Coalition for the Homeless, of trying to torpedo the work-training program that his own organization, the Doe Fund, runs for residents of the Harlem Men's Shelter. Banks, the Coalition's high-profile lawyer, countered that McDonald and the Doe Fund were exploiting the shelter residents by charging them $65 a week for rent. Dumbfounded by the charges and countercharges, the show's genial, ultraliberal host pleaded, "You're supposed to be on the same side. What's going on here?"

What's going on is a sea change in attitudes toward the homeless. The Coalition and other advocates remain wholly committed to the entitlement-oriented culture of the old shelter system, along with the belief that the cause of homelessness is a lack of affordable housing. But the Giuliani administration has other ideas. It has been contracting with tough-love programs like the Doe Fund to take over city homeless shelters, a new and, so far, quite successful approach that fundamentally challenges the old culture of dependency. Rejecting the Coalition's insistence that "housing, housing, housing" is the only solution for homelessness, George McDonald's program is based on the premise that the only real answer to the problem is work and personal responsibility. As McDonald recently told me, "My experience with homeless people has brought me to the conclusion that they are more capable of helping themselves than I thought, and than the advocates still think."

George McDonald's public challenge to the Coalition's entitlement philosophy and his unexpected emergence as an ally of the Giuliani administration represent a breathtaking 180-degree political turn. For no one, not even Steven Banks, has agitated more relentlessly in the trenches of the homeless-rights movement than he.

As a middle-class boy growing up in the quiet town of Spring Lake, New Jersey, in an area known as the Irish Riviera, McDonald had absorbed from the nuns who were his teachers an almost religious calling to help the poor. "They taught me," he recalls, "that other people's miseries are your miseries." In this spirit, in his mid-thirties, he abandoned a successful career as a sporting-goods-company executive for full-time social and political activism. A failed candidate during the 1980s in five races for Congress and one for City Council president, he ran each time on one main issue: homelessness. "In New York at the time," he says, "you could walk out of a restaurant after a $200 meal and have to step over a person on the street. The problem just stared you in the face."

By the mid-eighties McDonald had grown so obsessed with the homeless that he moved beyond mere advocacy into sharing his clients' lives. With his savings depleted and no steady source of income, he rented a six-by-nine-foot room in a single-room-occupancy hotel for $55 a week. As an unpaid volunteer for the Coalition for the Homeless, he spent most of his days and nights at Grand Central, feeding the homeless men and women camped out in the terminal's waiting rooms. Several times the Metro-North police arrested him for trespassing. He would also turn up at press conferences, looking shabby, to buttonhole reporters and politicians about the cause.

"I wanted to see what it was like to live in an SRO," McDonald says. "I had what I needed, and there were no distractions, and I was able to spend a lot of time getting the stories of the homeless out to the media. It also helped me, by immersion, figure out what the problem really consisted of. It was an incredibly liberating experience."

To the reporters covering the homeless beat, McDonald's views seemed no different from those of the Coalition's founder, Robert Hayes, who had brought the landmark 1979 *Callahan v. Carey* lawsuit against the city. The resulting consent decree called into being a vast, unprecedented gulag of drug- and crime-infested government shelters, at a per-person cost of more than $18,000 a year. Not that in the pre-*Callahan* days there was any shortage of places for people to go for basic sustenance: in addition to a few city-run shelters, there were voluntary agencies like the Salvation Army, and as a last resort, the city's welfare agency provided vouchers for Bowery-style flophouses. To Hayes and his allies, however, this improvised social safety net was inadequate and too uncertain. The unfortunate should not have to rely on the goodwill of the community, they said. Instead, in the time-honored fashion of advocates in New York, they purported to find an unqualified "right to shelter" in the State Constitution, which they succeeded in persuading the courts to enforce.

The Koch administration accepted the consent decree because it believed that an activist judiciary would rule against the city anyway and because many officials were sympathetic to Hayes's argument. Koch's former welfare commissioner William Grinker recalls: "At the time everyone in government thought that this was the right thing to do, that it was something that could be done. Only later was there this sense of, 'What did we get ourselves into?'" The estimated two thousand single homeless individuals in New York when the consent decree was signed had grown by the mid-1980s to an average of eleven thousand occupying city shelter beds on any given day, and as many as forty thousand who used the shelters at some time during the year.

Without a doubt, the consent decree created perverse incentives. Under it, the city couldn't test an applicant for drug or alcohol abuse or ask if he had any financial assets or alternative housing. "Once you make these kinds of guarantees and entitlements, people will use them," says Grinker. "And then it became an alternative living arrangement, even for some working people."

McDonald says that his own experiences in Grand Central made him realize that the remedies offered by the lawsuit were of little help to his homeless flock. "I never believed in the courts setting social policy on this issue," he insists. "I told Bob Hayes at the time that we had to have a political strategy that really did something for these people, that got them back on their feet and into the mainstream." After all, the Callahan for whom Hayes's famous lawsuit was named, an alcoholic who lived under an East River bridge, died on the streets despite Hayes's victory in court.

As one of the most active members of Mayor Dinkins's Commission on the Homeless, McDonald, along with commission chairman Andrew Cuomo, drafted its 1992 final report—the first official recognition that the policy of one-sided entitlements was a dismal failure. It acknowledged that most of the single adults in the shelters were not there for want of housing but because of drug addiction, mental illness, and other dysfunctional behavior. The report recommended that the city contract out management of its shelters to not-for-profit social service agencies and that a "balance of rights and responsibilities" be struck as part of a new "social contract" between the homeless and the city.

McDonald had learned the most important lesson of the streets and the shelters—that work and self-discipline, not whining about society's failings, were what these men needed most. "As a result of that experience, there definitely has been a shift in what I believe society has to do for a person, versus what that person has to do for himself," he says. "Now I know that if a guy gets a job, the housing pretty much can take care of itself."

McDonald contends—breaking once more with advocate orthodoxy—that New York, like the rest of America, offers his charges a sufficiency of jobs. "I believe that motivated people in the city of New York who are drug-free and reliable and show up every day for work can always find opportunity," McDonald told me. "Even with high unemployment rates and all the barriers our people have to overcome—prison records, substance-abuse episodes, and spotty employment

211

histories—still they wind up with jobs, because they are so motivated."

But, as Steven Banks suggested on the New York One program, aren't these jobs of the "dead-end" variety, leading nowhere? The concept infuriates McDonald: "Going to work, even picking up leaves or sweeping the streets, anybody who says that's a dead end doesn't have any understanding of the difference between the work culture—the free-enterprise culture—and the welfare culture. I mean, drugs lead to nowhere—to the grave. Yet the attitude of the advocates is, well, the homeless person has a right to lie on the street. The person has a right, a right, a right. That's our basic philosophical difference."

In 1985, McDonald created the Doe Fund—named for a homeless "Jane Doe" who died that year—and he began, in the Bedford-Stuyvesant section of Brooklyn, a small voluntary shelter program for homeless men based on the concept of personal responsibility. It enforced strict rules of behavior and offered both a mandatory work program, called "Ready, Willing & Able," and a serious job-search program. McDonald had contracted with the city's Housing Preservation and Development Department for the men in his program to do clean-up and small repairs in city-owned buildings. And when Andrew Cuomo joined the Clinton administration as an assistant secretary of Housing and Urban Development, McDonald received HUD grants for giving the homeless job training, along with recognition from Washington.

But when the new Giuliani administration faced its first budget crunch, McDonald found that the Doe Fund would lose almost a third of the $1.5 million it was receiving from city contracts. Instead of joining the long line of social service advocates at City Hall noisily protesting the "heartless" administration and its "devastating" budget cuts, he looked for a new market niche for his organization's services. As he observed the filthy condition of the streets and sidewalks near the fund's East 84th Street headquarters, a brainstorm came to him: why not have the men in the program clean the streets and then hope that the community would respond by helping to support that service? Soon crews from the Bedford-Stuyvesant shelter, dressed in neatly pressed blue jumpsuits, were sweeping up refuse along the Upper East Side's major arteries. Appreciative letters began arriving from local merchants and citizens, many with checks enclosed.

Two years ago the Giuliani administration began implementing the Cuomo Commission recommendations on turning over management of city shelters to not-for-profit organizations. In May 1996 it chose the Doe Fund to run the two-hundred-bed Harlem Men's Shelter, next to the Harlem River on the site of the old Polo Grounds. In less than a year McDonald transformed the shelter. Once filthy, drug-infested, and hopeless, it is now clean, drug-free, and a beehive of activity. By seven o'clock each morning the building has emptied out, with almost all the men off to their job assignments.

The *Callahan* consent decree is irrelevant to this human recovery community. The only mandate that counts is the contract that each man signs upon entering, laying out his obligations. After being confined to the shelter for a thirty-day orientation, during which he does odd jobs, gets a drug test, and sees both substance-abuse and job counselors, he goes to work full-time on one of the street-cleaning crews or a job assignment in city-owned buildings. If he successfully stays on this assignment during the nine to twelve months it takes to complete the program, and if he remains drug-free, he is likely to end up with a job, an apartment or room, and $2,000 in the bank, saved up for him by the shelter out of the $5.50 to $7 an hour in wages he earns from his work assignment.

213

The culture of the shelter stresses getting residents ready to join the workforce. In the evenings employment counselors help with résumés, interview preparation, and additional training. "If residents learn to stay sober, arrive at work on time, and keep a good attendance record, we can find them jobs," says Sharonann Smith, the fund's professional job developer. "There are a lot of companies that will hire them—not out of charity but because they want reliable workers."

Independent auditors confirm that over half the men who successfully complete the work program end up in regular paying jobs (most in the private sector) and in their own apartments. Graduates include an office assistant at K-III Communications Corporation, a $400-a-week cook at Beefsteak Charlie's, and a $14-an-hour construction worker at the Javits Convention Center. All this costs some $24,000 per resident per year, compared to the less than $20,000 the city spends in its own shelters. But the city pays the Doe Fund only $2.5 million per year, an average of about $13,000 per bed. McDonald's private fund-raising and his program's grants from the federal government make up the difference.

In my visits to the Harlem shelter, I met many men who had been hard-drug users living on the streets in truly desperate straits before they entered the program. Very few of them believed that they could make it back onto their feet without the program. One recent graduate, forty-seven-year-old Luther Harrison, is now a security guard at the Simon & Schuster building in midtown. He told me that he makes about $350 per week, has held the job steadily for almost two years, and lives in a Brooklyn apartment that he shares with a roommate. Before he went into the Doe Fund program, he had been in and out of various shelters and had spent some time living on the streets. "I was drinking and drugging, and I didn't have any self-esteem," he told me. "Finally I got fed up with being homeless. Enough is enough."

I spoke to one Doe Fund worker who was cleaning up my street corner on the West Side, another neighborhood where McDonald's troops now work. A thirty-one-year-old black man named Miles Burke, he had graduated from Thomas Jefferson High School in Brooklyn and then served in the army. After his discharge he got into drugs and crime and ended up serving four years on a felony conviction. After his release he was back on the streets and on drugs again. He spent some time in the shelters, and some in Central Park or on the subways, supporting himself by panhandling and shoplifting. With his life spinning out of control, he heard about the Doe Fund from a relative.

"I was tired," he told me. "I had enough of that kind of life." Now he was up every day at 5:30. By 7:30 he was on Amsterdam Avenue cleaning up and bagging garbage. Working until 3:30, he then headed back to the shelter for his computer classes and Narcotics Anonymous sessions. He was already sending out applications for civil service jobs and for public housing. "I can't be dependent on the Doe Fund," he said. "Eventually you have to leave the shelter and make it on your own. I am not a victim of society or anything like that. I just made some bad choices. But it's the nineties now, and I have my chances to do something for myself."

Out on the streets with the cleaning crews, you can feel the radical cultural impact the program makes. While Miles Burke cleans the street and bags garbage, other homeless men stand in front of stores and banks, shaking their Styrofoam cups and looking for a handout. It has been my impression, however—shared by local storekeepers—that there are fewer of them since the Doe Fund cleaning crews arrived. Could it be that with some homeless men really *working* in public spaces, it has become more untenable for others to "work" the streets in the old manner?

Programs like the Doe Fund suggest that the rotten edifice created by the consent decree and by organizations such as the Coalition for the Homeless is tottering and needs only a well-placed push. Maybe now, at the end of a first Giuliani administration that has so effectively recast the terms of the city's welfare reform debate, there really is a golden opportunity to end the destructive regime of homeless class rights imposed by the courts.

As George McDonald puts it: "When the history of this issue is written, it will be judged a profound failure that social policy in New York City was set by judges and courts—a profound failure and an incredible waste of resources. Think of all the money that's gone down this rat hole of a shelter system that could have been spent in actually getting people out of the conditions they were in." He knows whereof he speaks.

[1997]

KAY S. HYMOWITZ

At Last, a Job Program
That Works

THE NEW ERA of welfare reform is here, but one of its most vexing questions has yet to be answered: how to move the inexperienced and unskilled into the workplace. Little in the history of welfare-to-work programs encourages much optimism on the subject—though not for lack of money or effort. In 1995 alone, the federal government appropriated $20 billion for 163 different programs. The giant carcasses of failed federal programs like CETA, the Manpower Development and Training Act, the Job Corps, and most recently, JOBS, litter the landscape. As urban ethnologist Elijah Anderson has described job-training programs, they are little more than "human holding cells."

That dark background makes the success of Strive, a

break-the-mold job-readiness program utterly unlike government-funded programs, all the more luminous. With its central office in a part of East Harlem so drug-ridden that it was dubbed "the devil's playground," Strive targets an even tougher population than other job-readiness programs: 25 percent of its clients are ex-offenders, many have a history of prolonged drug use, some are tentatively housed or even homeless, half are on welfare, and almost all have been victims of the New York City public schools.

But while other programs focus on "hard skills" like computer literacy, word processing, and job-search techniques, Strive's staff is skeptical about such instruction. Instead, convinced that employers want to hire eager, presentable workers and are willing to train them once on the job, Strive staffers concentrate on building what they see as the all-important "soft skills": not just the familiar problems of initiative and punctuality but a more subtle understanding of the manners and values of an alien mainstream work world.

If such a Pygmalion change in a mere three weeks seems impossible, consider the results. At its nineteen sites in New York, Boston, Pittsburgh, and Chicago, Strive has put almost fourteen thousand people, 35 to 40 percent of them men, to work during a five-year period, at the modest cost of $1,500 each. More striking still, where most programs count themselves successful if participants are working after a final three-month follow-up, Strive, whose other defining characteristic is a lifetime commitment to clients, has been able to ensure that close to 80 percent of those placed are still working after *two years.*

The simple reason for Strive's success is that the program's staff, whose truly disadvantaged histories resemble those of their clients, have themselves traveled the gulf between the street culture their clients now inhabit and the office culture they seek to join. Their firsthand view of this gap corresponds closely to the picture that emerges from the pages of sociologist William Julius Wilson's recent, highly touted book *When Work Disappears*. In interviews with 179 Cook County firms offering entry-level jobs, Wilson shows that employers—both black and white—often find inner-city workers, particularly males, uncooperative, prickly, undependable, and lacking in initiative. What about lack of job skills, which, according to conventional wisdom, is the primary roadblock to employment? Fewer than 12 percent of the employers interviewed cited it as a major problem.

The staff at Strive are hardly the first to note the difficulty many inner-city residents have adapting to the requirements of the workplace. What makes them unique is their sophisticated grasp of the psychology behind this well-known, if widely denied, problem. Without scorn or pity, they see through the self-defeating postures their clients have adopted, postures that dramatize their indignant sense of racial exclusion and perpetuate their marginalization. These "roles of the stoop and the street," as one staffer puts it, are familiar and predictable: for some clients it is passivity, for others it is racial blaming, for many it is the strut of "attitude." By vigorously confronting these almost stereotypical postures and providing support in understanding alternatives, Strive's staff offer the disadvantaged a more solid bridge to the mainstream work world than the usual approaches of the "don't-blame-the-victim" social worker, the "fill-in-the-blanks" bureaucrat, and the "sink-or-swim" libertarian.

Some people hear about Strive from friends, neighbors, drug counselors, or parole officers, but the majority find the program through an ad in the *Daily News*. No matter where they come from, recruits can't possibly be prepared for what they will witness during the three-hour orientation. Utterly

219

unlike conventional job training, it is stunning theater, a hybrid of comedy club, encounter group, and Republican campaign speech. Rob Carmona, the executive director of the program, who seems equally comfortable in Armani in the corporate dining room or in "homeboy" jeans in the project courtyard, has taken off his suit jacket and paces back and forth in front of the sixty men and women. He launches into the major themes of the program with the barely suppressed urgency that will energize the weeks to come.

"How come not one bodega around here is owned by a Puerto Rican?" he demands. "Not one. They used to be all Puerto Rican. Now the Puerto Ricans are too proud to work in a bodega, and so they're all owned by Dominicans. These people come from places where, if you don't work, you don't eat. . . . More important in life than intelligence is emotional maturity. And I'm tellin' it like it is: people of color have lost it!" Some in the audience watch suspiciously; others nod their heads and exclaim quietly, "Tell it!" or "It's the truth!"

Carmona does not let go for a full half-hour. "When I was on drugs in the sixties, I would always blame it on whitey. Your building smells? I got news for you: the people pissin' in hallways are not some white guys from New Jersey." Later he challenges a woman who is radiating hostility, one of the few people older than thirty in the group: "I can't believe you've taken this attitude in front of eighteen-year-olds. What kind of model are you? That's why our community is in so much trouble."

While this cold shower of personal-responsibility talk is the mainstay of the program, no one at Strive is naive about the disadvantages burdening many clients. Anyone needing advice about child care or housing, or help negotiating with city agencies, will get it from Strive personnel. Still, clients will be warned repeatedly: "I'm sorry for your problems. But you cannot bring them to work." If the staff seems insensitive, as some have accused, that's because they see their clients not as damaged victims but as mature adults who, with a bit of help, can find a way to cope. And as adults they can be told the truth. "The world is changing out there," Carmona almost shouts. "Wake up! Come July 1, no one is going to come up to you and say, 'Luis, gee, before we cut you off welfare, do you have everything you need?' Ain't nothing sensitive about it. That's reality!"

Nor is the staff Pollyannish about racism. The associate director and trainer at Strive's West Harlem site, Steve Berlack, was plucked out of his South Bronx home at fourteen to become a scholarship student at Andover, where he experienced precisely the sort of culture shock he trains his clients to negotiate. He warns them that they'll find people in the mainstream world who believe African-Americans are not as capable as whites or other minorities. But the proper response, he tells them, is not to become hostile or make excuses. As Rob Carmona tells the group, if anyone experiences what seems to be unjust treatment on the job, the correct response is to "sit back, suck it in, and call us. Don't quit your job. You can't tell your kids there's no milk in the refrigerator because the world is racist." One young man in the group I followed will be told to tone down the "vibes which say 'angry black man.'" All will be encouraged repeatedly to see themselves through the eyes of employers. "It is your job to make yourself liked," Carmona pronounces.

According to these trainers, the real problem isn't discrimination but "attitude," the quasi-defensive, quasi-aggressive posture their clients have adopted to anticipate discrimination. Shelby Steele has called this double-edged self-presentation "the bite of the underdog." Yes, occasionally you will meet with racists and racism, is the Strive message,

221

but don't spend all your energy waiting for it—even looking for it. As Berlack points out to his charges: "Life is 10 percent what happens to you—and 90 percent how you react." Carmona offers the story of driving his wife's new Jeep in his suburban neighborhood and being approached by a policeman. "Oh, shit—excuse my English—he sees me here, a black man in my homeboy clothes in a shiny new car in Teaneck. I'm thinkin': 'Here it comes, here it comes.' And you know what he says? He says, 'Nice car. Is that the new Toyota Rav?'" He sums up: "We make assumptions about what's gonna come at us. Whether we like or not, we got attitude."

Strive's focus on "attitude" cuts to the deepest truths about inner-city joblessness. At its crudest, the welfare debate has sounded like an argument between those who believe that poor minorities are lazy and don't want to work and those who think they really want to work but simply can't find jobs. Strive's experience casts doubt on both positions. As many close observers of ghetto life like William Julius Wilson and Elijah Anderson have remarked, inner-city residents at least state a belief in the importance of hard work and personal initiative. In fact, the people who come to Strive are obsessed with finding jobs and are tearfully grateful to the staff when they do so—the office is filled with mushy thank-you notes, stuffed animals, balloons, and other gifts of appreciation.

Still, Wilson's theory—that though inner-city people want jobs, the only kind of work for which they are qualified has "disappeared"—is also at odds with Strive's experience. The main disjunction Strive's staff members see is that between the values of the street and those of the mainstream work world. Socialized to the norms of street honor, their clients are imprisoned in failure by a reluctance to accept the alien atmosphere and petty humiliations inevitable at almost any workplace. It would not surprise Strive's staff to learn from urban ethnologist Philippe Bourgois, who studied the crack subculture on the very blocks around Strive's East Harlem site, that when some of his subjects were fired from legitimate jobs, they would treat their return to the street "as a triumph of free will and resistance." As the opposite face of the same coin, many successful Strive participants have had the experience of Zakeina, one former welfare mother I spoke with, whose friend warned her to quit the program because she had begun "acting white" and "putting on airs."

During the orientation, Berlack, who has the comic timing and talent for mimicry of Eddie Murphy, uses his experience in the army to drive home the theme of "attitude." Suddenly and unexpectedly, he screams hysterically to a young woman whom he has been teasing in the front of the room: "Duck!" She flinches in shocked surprise. In the riff that follows, he mimics a stereotypic black street tough. He ambles forward in what Tom Wolfe has called the "pimp roll" and says in a heavy accent: "'Who you tellin' to duck? Ain't nobody goin' to tell me what to do. I don't duck for no one.' And you know what happens to that guy?" Berlack has returned to his usual Andover-smooth English with just a hint of a Southern accent. "He's dead meat, because there's a bullet flying by, and he 'don't take no orders from no one.'"

During the three weeks of the workshop, the seriousness underlying this comedy grows increasingly clear. Early on, prospective participants are warned that they are being tested: "Strive is not a democracy. Adhere to our rules or leave." Some will; by Monday the sixty people at Friday's orientation have dwindled to forty.

But merely showing up is not enough. Day after day, staffers will challenge those who need it to recognize the depth of their resistance to authority and to repress its subtle symptoms—bored facial expressions, smirks, slouching, and almost unconscious clucks of disgust. At one session Gloria, a usually quiet twenty-three-year-old, complains that the group was not given enough instruction to complete the day's assignment. At first one wonders if the trainers are being too harsh when they prod her. "Did you ask yourself, what is your role in this?" they badger. "Did you show some initiative? Did you ask us to clarify?" But then trainer Frank Horton calls attention to the way Gloria is sitting. She is leaning back in her chair with her arms crossed over her chest—just the kind of subtle gesture of "you-can't-tell-me-what-to-do" defiance bound to irritate a supervisor on the job.

At another session a woman argues about the size of her earrings: "earrings no larger than a quarter" is one of Strive's many pieces of advice for job interviews. She takes out a quarter to make her point. A long, seemingly trivial discussion ensues, but by the end of it the rest of the group has joined the trainer to disagree with her. "This wasn't just about earrings," a trainer tells me later. "It's about teamwork and learning to accept authority. This woman told us she has lost three jobs because she couldn't get along with her supervisors. If we don't break her down, she'll lose the next one too. She needs to know that, and so do the others." And as if on cue, one man, challenged after failing to complete an assignment from the trainers because he had "personal business," stalks out during the first week. "I don't kiss ass, I get ass!" he blusters, demonstrating the truth of Horton's insight that while most of Strive's ghetto participants value the "expensive commodity" of street pride, it is especially treasured by men.

Pride and the prickliness it causes in the face of criticism and instruction are not the only self-defeating qualities in the repertory of Strive's minority clients. The staff is on the watch for other sorts of self-damaging behavior. As assistant trainer Joelle James explains after Michelle, a giggly, prattling eighteen-year-old, goes crying to Horton when her silliness is confronted: "Although we deal with about forty people every month, they're the same people with different faces. There are patterns. For instance, Michelle is immature, undisciplined. She is used to crying to get her way, particularly with men. We've seen her before."

Trainers have also seen plenty of "my-life-is-a-mess-but-it's-not-my-fault" victim playing. Because Strive is determined to inspire a sense of their clients' power to control their own lives, they question any excuses for past failure, no matter how seemingly justified. As one trainer explains: "We tell them, 'Your job as an employee is to make yourself indispensable. If there are layoffs, you shouldn't be the one. You have to do more than the job.'" Says manager of job development Daniel Jusino, whose voice, even once in his office, never falls below a shout: "If they complain about the government, we say, 'Did you vote?' If the building smells, we say, 'What are you doing about it?' If they say, 'I couldn't work, I'm a mother'"—he puffs out his chest in prideful imitation—"we'll say, 'What kind of mother are you, when you can't pay the rent?'"

Shyness is another familiar pattern in the Strive cast of clients, some of whom are so quiet they seem to have closed the door and pulled their egos in with them. Everyone is required not only to speak to a video camera for five full minutes in the first week but to participate actively in all parts of the workshop. When a young woman averts her head coyly as she stands up to answer a question, Horton imitates her. "I don't need the pose," he tells her. At another session, Berlack calls forward a good-looking, lanky eighteen-year-old named Corey. "Y'all know Corey," he says, gently mimicking the way the boy, hands in pockets, looks down at his scuffling feet. "He stands around the projects with the other guys, and the girls

225

come over, and, gosh, they think he's so sweet." The women in the group, myself included, burst out laughing. Now here's a real familiar character.

Embarrassing as this encounter was for Corey, it is actually a key test: will the young man react with anger or yet more passivity, or will he begin to shed his defensive armor? Because Strive depends on the satisfaction of its pool of employers, its job developers cannot risk recommending people who do not live up to their standards of maturity and responsibility. Though they accept almost all comers, the success of their business requires weeding out the intractably hostile, immature, and withdrawn. Typically, after the initial 35 percent falloff following the three-hour orientation, about 6 percent more leave during the three-week workshop; in the one group I watched, the twenty-one starters dwindled to sixteen by the last week.

Corey will be one of those who do not make it. His story offers an abstract of the strengths and limitations of Strive's unyielding approach. In the third week the clients, who have gradually come to understand that their own futures are at stake in the reputation of the organization, are asked whether he should graduate. He has failed to participate, and even when they beg him to speak up, he can only mutter, "I'm not sure" or "I don't know." They reluctantly, even tearfully, conclude that he shouldn't graduate, though they remind him that he can come back and try again. Strive's attitude toward the Coreys, the Michelles, and the "I don't kiss ass" blusterers of this world is not that they are hopeless failures, but only that they are unready for the character transformation asked of them.

Another, more familiar character the staff watches out for is the addict. At every workshop at least half the participants have been drug or alcohol abusers; any current addicts are referred to rehabilitation programs. Strive is extremely strict about even casual drug use. "Don't think you can smoke a joint on the weekend and get away with it," they warn their clients in a tough but necessary rule. Almost all of Strive's employers test for drugs, and some go so far as to take hair samples for a more reliable reading. The organization has been able to help its employer pool avoid the results of one Chicago boss quoted by William Julius Wilson, who estimates he has had to disqualify 30 percent of his inner-city black hires after drug screening.

On the surface, the second and third weeks of Strive's program resemble more traditional job training. The participants work to complete their résumés and to polish up interview skills. When I arrive for the big day of the mock interview, the transformation of the group from the initial week is striking. Gone are the short skirts, baggy pants, flashy jewelry, and dreadlocks, along with the slouching, the yawning, and the crossed arms. Now the women are wearing blouses and jackets, knee-length skirts, simple gold chains and small earrings, stockings and heels; the men, dark pants and jackets with white shirts and understated ties. (Strive keeps a room of "gently used" clothing for those unable to afford appropriate interview wear.) Everyone is sitting straight up, the women with legs crossed at the ankles, their hands in their laps.

Yet underlying the professional surface is a palpable air of anxiety. In part, it is the anticipation of venturing alone into an unfamiliar, even exotic, new land. But it is also the anxiety of "racial vulnerability" described so exquisitely by Shelby Steele in *The Content of Our Character*. Stripped of self-justifying inertia and the mask of "attitude," presenting themselves as individuals rather than as members of a victimized group, the sixteen participants left in the room have nothing to protect them from their underlying fear of failure, a fear, as Steele sees it, fueled by the historical myth of their inferiority.

Mona, a twenty-nine-year-old who, like the others, has had eight days to prepare for her interview, has just shaken hands with the job developers posing as employers and is now shifting uneasily in her seat. When asked why she thinks she should get the job, she awkwardly stalls for time. "That's a good question," she stammers, but then her hands fly to her face and she shakes her head. "I had it. I had it," she whimpers. Her nervousness might touch an outsider, but Jusino is not interested in "feeling-land," as he calls it. He barks a series of questions at the young woman: "What's your date of birth? What's your Social Security number? What's your phone number? How come you weren't nervous when you answered those questions? Because you've been answering them your whole life. When you say things a thousand times, you're not nervous. Practice. Repetition, people: that's the key to preparing for the interview."

This preparation for the journey from uptown to downtown, small in actual miles but immense in psychological distance, clearly works. A random sampling of twenty employers by New York University found that 90 percent of them remarked on the confidence displayed during the interview, as well as the general motivation and good attitude of Strive graduates. Flo Robinson, personnel recruiter for Mt. Sinai Hospital, is not unusual. "Their résumés are complete, and they follow up on every part of the application without complaining. If you ask me, they often seem better prepared than people with master's degrees."

Strive's funders, the largest of which is the Clark Foundation, range from the left-wing Aaron Diamond Foundation to the conservative Smith Richardson Foundation. But the organization doesn't take government money, believing that the strings attached to it strangle just those qualities that led to

Strive's commendation by the Government Accounting Office in 1996 as one of six job-training programs in the U.S. that work. For instance, says Rob Carmona, because of how the government pays its job-training providers, "If a person drops out, you don't get paid. It's your goal to keep that person at all costs, so you make excuses for him every day, even if you know he's going out and smoking a joint during lunch." One thirty-five-year-old woman confirmed this picture during a lunch break at Strive: "I've been to other job-training programs, and they're not strict enough. They just smile nice at you."

This contrast with other programs helps put Strive's sometimes abrasive toughness in a different light. If, unlike many programs, it demands a great deal of emotional endurance from its participants, it is also unlike those programs in giving much support in return. Remember that Strive's commitment is for life. "We don't see the loss of the first job as a failure but as a developmental tool," says Carmona. Horton elaborates: "Some of our people get their first paychecks and they're high. Then their demons start to whisper in their ear. 'Hey, this isn't much money; what am I working so hard for?' They get insubordinate and get fired, or the employer calls us. We send them back to the workshop to get recooked." But clients don't need to fail in order to receive more help from Strive. They can come back to practice on computers—the office is open on Saturdays—to get help in finding a new job, to plan the next stage in their careers.

Strive has recently instituted a new program for higher-level job training, but its staff makes no apologies for their basic "there-is-no-better-training-for-work-than-work" philosophy. Given the background of their clientele, they encourage a hard-nosed realism about their immediate opportunities. Jusino tells the group in the middle of the first week: "There are lots of programs out there that'll sell you dreams:

229

you can be an astronaut or something. We don't sell you dreams. I guarantee you, if you follow the program, we'll get you a job making more than you are making now. That's all."

Irving Brown, who has hired more than fifty Strive graduates over the past year for his company, Choice Courier, confirms the success of this lesson. "Strive people understand what's expected of them, and you don't have to reinvent them. They understand that this is a job to give them discipline and basic skills, which they can translate into a more meaningful job in the future. They know they're captains of their own fate. Of the people I've hired, I'd say 75 percent are still here after a year, and the others have gone on to better positions."

In his final book, sociologist Christopher Lasch argued for an "ethos of respect" to supplant what he saw as the prevailing "ethos of compassion" toward the poor. Underlying the prodding, teasing, and confrontation, it is just this kind of respect that Strive displays toward its clients. Insisting on realism, plainspokenness, and clear, impersonal standards of conduct, its staff members neither patronize nor condescend, for they truly believe in the capacities of their clients. Lasch went on in the same book to call compassion, at least in its contemporary American form, "the human face of contempt," and the Strive approach helps explain the truth of this harsh aphorism. Rather than merely pitying the poor as victims and thereby reinforcing their helplessness, Strive instead believes in their competence and appeals to their ability to climb atop their miserable circumstances and see new possibilities. It's a tough climb, but for those willing and able to make it, it works wonders.

[1997]

A Note on Contributors

BRIAN C. ANDERSON is senior editor of *City Journal* and the author of *Raymond Aron: The Recovery of the Political*. His writings have appeared in *First Things, The Wilson Quarterly,* and *The Public Interest*.

HOWARD HUSOCK is director of case studies at Harvard's John F. Kennedy School of Government and a *City Journal* contributing editor. An Emmy Award–winning journalist, he is the author of *Repairing the Ladder: Towards a New Housing Policy Paradigm*. He has also written for the *Wall Street Journal* and *The Public Interest*.

KAY S. HYMOWITZ, a contributing editor of *City Journal*, is the author of *Ready or Not: Why Treating Children as Small Adults Endangers Their Future and Ours*. She has written for the *Wall Street Journal, The New Republic,* and the *New York Times*.

HEATHER MAC DONALD is a contributing editor of *City Journal* and John M. Olin Fellow at the Manhattan Institute. Her articles have appeared in the *Wall Street Journal, The New Republic, The New Criterion,* and the *New York Times*.

MYRON MAGNET is editor of *City Journal* and author of *The Dream and the Nightmare: The Sixties' Legacy to the Underclass*.

A Note on Contributors

SOL STERN, a contributing editor of *City Journal*, has written for *Commentary*, the *Wall Street Journal*, and the *New York Times*, and has served as a policy analyst for the governments of New York City and New York State.

WILLIAM J. STERN is a contributing editor of *City Journal*. He chaired New York governor Mario Cuomo's 1982 campaign and from 1983 to 1985 headed the state's Urban Development Corporation.

LEO TRACHTENBERG, a former documentary filmmaker, writes for the publication department of the New York Yankees. He is the author of a history of the 1927 Yankees, *The Wonder Team*.

Index

Index

Index

Index

Index

Index

O'Grady, John, 25
Olasky, Marvin, 112
Olin Foundation, 147
Ollennu, Osmond, 89–90
"One Church, One Child," 63
100 neediest cases (*New York Times*), 124–144; cases of 1912, 127; cases of 1921, 127–128; cases of 1929, 129; cases of 1933, 129; cases of 1940s, 130–132, 133; cases of 1950s, 134; cases of 1960s, 134–136; cases of 1970s, 137–139; cases of 1980s, 139–140; cases of 1990s, 132, 139–144
Orphan Asylum (New York), 46
Other America, The (Harrington), 134
Outline of a New System of Physiognomy (Redfield), 13
Outward Bound, 107
Oxford Movement, 27–28

Parsons, Ralph, 13
Pecora, Peter, 45
Pena, Luz, 142
Pencil (Public Education Needs Civic Involvement in Learning), 191
Personal responsibility, 15, 19, 34, 64, 82–83, 120, 220–221
Peter J. Dellamonica Center for Seniors, 119
Peterson, Robert, 95
Philadelphia, 6–7; Jewish immigrants in, 41–68; textile industry, 48
Philadelphia Evening Ledger, 60
Philadelphia Hospital for Mental Diseases (Byeberry), 50
Philadelphia-wide Association for Jewish Children, 67
Philanthropy, 145–171; advocacy and litigation, 165–171; collaborative movements in, 161–165; diversity and, 146,

157–161; liberal versus conservative, 147; race and, 146, 157–158; scientific philanthropy versus scientific socialism, 148, 149. *See also* Charity.
Pifer, Alan, 146, 156
Pittsburgh, 218
Pius IX (pope), 29
Plain Talk, 161–164
Plepler, Richard, 204
Polk, Davis, 188
Poverty: deserving versus undeserving poor, 125, 175; entitlement, 130; illegitimacy and, 128, 141–142; juvenile delinquency and, 130, 131; 100 neediest cases (*New York Times*), 124–144; pro bono legal work and, 173–174, 175; psychoanalytic model, 131–132; self-destructive behavior and, 143–144; self-fulfillment and, 131
Poverty law, 179–180
Powell, Robert Baden, 91–92
Presley, Elvis, 134
Primedia, 192
Prisoners' rights, 167–168, 185, 187
Pro bono legal work, 172–189; conservative cases, 188–189; currently, 181–189; early history of, 172–180
Progressives, 174, 187
Prostate cancer, 56–57
Protectory News, 38
Protestant ministers, 7
Psychoanalytic model, 131–132
Public health nursing, 69–88
Public Welfare Foundation, 166
Pugh, Kathi, 189

Race and racism: Catholic Charities and, 113–114; against the Irish, 6, 13; jobs and, 221–222; philanthropy and, 146, 157–158

240

Index